REGIONAL COOKING OF INDIA

REGIONAL COOKING OF INDIA

80 RECIPES, SHOWN IN 350 EXQUISITE PHOTOGRAPHS

MRIDULA
BALJEKAR

Photography by Jon Whitaker

aqua marine

This edition is published by Aquamarine, an imprint of
Anness Publishing Ltd, Hermes House, 88-89 Blackfriars Road, London SE1 8HA;
tel. 020 7401 2077; fax 020 7633 9499

www.aquamarinebooks.com; www.annesspublishing.com

If you like the images in this book and would like to investigate using them for publishing, promotions or advertising, please visit our website www.practicalpictures.com for more information.

UK agent: The Manning Partnership Ltd; tel. 01225 478444;
fax 01225 478440; sales@manning-partnership.co.uk
UK distributor: Book Trade Services; tel. 0116 2759086; fax 0116 2759090;
uksales@booktradeservices.com; exportsales@booktradeservices.com
North American agent/distributor: National Book Network;
tel. 301 459 3366; fax 301 429 5746; www.nbnbooks.com
Australian agent/distributor: Pan Macmillan Australia; tel. 1300 135 113;
fax 1300 135 103; customer.service@macmillan.com.au
New Zealand agent/distributor: David Bateman Ltd;
tel. (09) 415 7664; fax (09) 415 8892

Publisher: Joanna Lorenz
Editorial Director: Helen Sudell
Project Editors: Catherine Stuart, Melanie Hibbert
Desk Editor: Barbara Toft
Designer: Gabriella Le Grazie
Photography: Jon Whitaker
Food Stylist: Joy Skipper
Prop Stylist: Penny Markham
Proofreading Manager: Lindsay Zamponi
Production Controller: Claire Rae

PUBLISHER'S NOTE

Although the advice and information in this book are believed to be accurate and true at the time of going to press, neither the authors nor the publisher can accept any legal responsibility or liability for any errors or omissions that may be made.

PICTURE ACKNOWLEDGEMENTS:

The publisher would like to thank Jon Whitaker for his stunning photography throughout the book, apart from the following images: Corbis pages 6, 7, 8, 10, 11b, 12, 13, 14 ; Getty Images page 11t, iStockphoto page 9t and Matt Munro for author portrait on the jacket.

ETHICAL TRADING POLICY

At Anness Publishing we believe that business should be conducted in an ethical and ecologically sustainable way, with respect for the environment and a proper regard to the replacement of the natural resources we employ.

As a publisher, we use a lot of wood pulp to make high-quality paper for printing, and that wood commonly comes from spruce trees. We are therefore currently growing more than 750,000 trees in three Scottish forest plantations: Berrymoss (130 hectares/320 acres), West Touxhill (125 hectares/305 acres) and Deveron Forest (75 hectares/185 acres). The forests we manage contain more than 3.5 times the number of trees employed each year in making paper for the books we manufacture.

Because of this ongoing ecological investment programme, you, as our customer, can have the pleasure and reassurance of knowing that a tree is being cultivated on your behalf to naturally replace the materials used to make the book you are holding.

Our forestry programme is run in accordance with the UK Woodland Assurance Scheme (UKWAS) and will be certified by the internationally recognized Forest Stewardship Council (FSC). The FSC is a non-government organization dedicated to promoting responsible management of the world's forests. Certification ensures forests are managed in an environmentally sustainable and socially responsible way. For further information about this scheme, go to www.annesspublishing.com/trees

NOTES

- Bracketed terms are intended for American readers.
- For all recipes, quantities are given in both metric and imperial measures and, where appropriate, in standard cups and spoons. Follow one set of measures, but not a mixture, because they are not interchangeable.
- Standard spoon and cup measures are level. 1 tsp = 5ml, 1 tbsp = 15ml, 1 cup = 250ml/8fl oz.
- Australian standard tablespoons are 20ml. Australian readers should use 3 tsp in place of 1 tbsp for measuring small quantities of gelatine, flour, salt, etc.
- American pints are 16fl oz/2 cups. American readers should use 20fl oz/2.5 cups in place of 1 pint when measuring liquids.
- Electric oven temperatures in this book are for conventional ovens. When using a fan oven, the temperature will probably need to be reduced by about 10-20°C/20-40°F. Since ovens vary, you should check with your manufacturer's instruction book for guidance.
- The nutritional analysis given for each recipe is calculated per portion (i.e. serving or item), unless otherwise stated. If the recipe gives a range, such as Serves 4-6, then the nutritional analysis will be for the smaller portion size, i.e. 6 servings. Measurements for sodium do not include salt added to taste.
- Medium (US large) eggs are used unless otherwise stated.

CONTENTS

Introduction

Indian dishes are possibly among the most popular in the world. Brightly coloured vegetables in richly flavoured sauces; tender meat, poultry and fish; nutty-flavoured beans and lentils; and of course, an incredible array of spices epitomize an exciting cuisine that warms the body and soothes the spirit. Besides offering fabulous flavours Indian cooking is extremely healthy, with the emphasis being firmly on freshness. Some popular ingredients are even believed to have medicinal properties.

The vast and vibrant land of India conjures up images of mystery, magic and romance. It is a land steeped in heritage and history, one that has witnessed great empires rise and crumble.

Exotic spices have been grown in India for centuries, and it is carefully prepared blends of these spices that provide the mouthwatering tastes, flavours and aromas of countless dishes eaten throughout the entire country.

India has long been known as the spice bowl of the world. The use of premium quality spices in this sun-drenched, monsoon-fed land was an established way of life long before the traders arrived. Among those lured to the country by the valuable spices were Arabs, English, Dutch, Portuguese and Spanish.

Foreign travellers introduced cooking styles that are still practised today. The north continues to be dominated by Mughal cuisine, while the east has tribal and Anglo-Indian styles. In the south, Syrian Jews and French traders passed on their cooking techniques, and western India came under the influence of the Portuguese and the Persians (Parsis). The result is a rich, colourful and multi-dimensional cuisine with a repertoire of recipes that is virtually unmatched anywhere else in the world.

Spectacular scenery, fascinating ancient customs and glorious foods all continue to draw foreigners to this magical land. Just like the breathtakingly beautiful scenery, culinary traditions have also been influenced by geographical and climatic conditions. With vast distances to be travelled, and no means of transporting fresh produce efficiently, cooks have made the best use of the ingredients available to them locally.

Rice or breads form the staple diet in India. Meat and fish are served in small quantities, surrounded by inviting little side dishes, such as pickles, chutneys and salads. Enticing recipes are flavoured with fresh herbs and chillies, yogurt or soy sauce. Many of the ingredients used in these dishes are known for their healing powers. For example, there is strong evidence that garlic and fresh root ginger, two of the most essential ingredients in curries, contain properties that can help to combat heart diseases and stomach ulcers respectively.

The beauty of Indian cooking is in its variety. Different areas and traditions have developed their own regional specialities, and recipes have been handed down through the generations. Although many Indian dishes are fiery with chillies, there are others that are mellow. Many of the most familiar regional dishes we enjoy come from northern India. These include koftas, mild kormas and tandoori recipes. Balti cuisine, which is Kashmiri cooking from the area that is now north Pakistan, is beautifully aromatic, but does not use chillies excessively, so it is not too hot. The most fiery spice blends, such as the famous vindaloo, come from western India. Coconuts are favourite ingredients of

LEFT Fresh produce such as herbs and vegetables are important ingredients and are sold in open air markets.

ABOVE Clay-oven-baked tandoori dishes originate from the north of India but their mild flavours are enjoyed worldwide.

ABOVE A typical vegetarian Indian meal from Kerala in southern India, made up of a variety of small dishes.

ABOVE Balti cuisine takes its name from the heavy-based dish in which it is traditionally cooked and served.

eastern and southern India, and are used for making both sweet and savoury dishes, including deliciously creamy sauces. From western India there are recipes that use dairy products including yogurt and buttermilk, and the meals are typically accompanied by all kinds of unusual pickles. As south Indian cuisine is predominantly vegetarian, there is no shortage of delectable meat-free recipes to choose from, which utilize nuts, beans, peas and lentils, making hearty and nutritious meals to appeal to vegetarians and meat-eaters.

The book is divided into regional sections that represent the best of the different cuisines of India, from soups and appetizers to fish and shellfish dishes, meat, poultry and vegetable dishes. It also includes a variety of side dishes, salads, chutneys and relishes, as well as breads, desserts and drinks – in fact everything you need to create the perfect meal, whether it be a simple evening supper or a more elaborate dinner party for friends and family.

Many recipes are quick to prepare with the simplest of spice combinations, whereas others call for a more varied store of spices and flavourings, including some lesser-known ingredients, such as mango powder (amchur) and compressed tamarind. Today most of these special ingredients are readily available from supermarkets as well as health-food stores. Fresh herbs such as coriander (cilantro) are sold cheaply in large bunches in Asian stores and markets. These stores also sell large bags of whole spices which will provide you with a plentiful supply for flavouring all your favourite Indian dishes and are ideal if you enjoy preparing spicy food regularly.

Many of the culinary skills and expertise widely used around the world today were originally developed in India, and a selection of the best of Indian regional cuisine is featured in this wonderful collection of uncomplicated recipes.

RIGHT With its many and varied side dishes, an Indian meal is perfect for sharing with friends and family.

A land of contrasts

The variations in the regional cuisine of modern-day India may not be as pronounced as they once were, but in a country so vast it is inevitable that long-standing traditions for produce and cooking styles have persisted. India is an incredibly varied land, both geographically and climatically, from the mighty snow-clad Himalayas in the extreme north to the wonderfully fertile flatlands of the Indus and Ganges rivers, and the dry and sandy wastes of the deserts of Rajasthan.

Rugged north

The states of Himachal Pradesh, Jammu, Kashmir, the Punjab and Uttar Pradesh make up northern India. The highest mountain range in the world, the Himalayas stretch majestically from the rugged north-west to the river Brahmaputra in the east. The valleys of the Himalayas are famous for growing exquisite basmati rice and sugar cane.

The magnificent mountains stand in stunning contrast to lush green valleys dotted with lakes, where the mighty river Indus flows. Recipes based on lamb or succulent, firm-fleshed river fish of various kinds are favourites in northern India. Trees are laden with sweet, juicy plums, peaches, rich red cherries, almonds and walnuts, and these feature regularly in many mouthwatering sweet and savoury dishes of the northern regions.

Tropical south

Southern India conjures up visions of swaying coconut palm trees, golden beaches and lush tropical scenery. The states of Andhra Pradesh, Tamil Nadu, Karnataka and Kerala make up south India. Each of these states is rich in history and heritage and has its own typical culinary traditions and styles.

Here in the south, the Deccan plateau is kept lush and fertile by two major rivers. In the state of Karnataka the landscape is varied, with smooth, sandy beaches, rugged mountains, winding rivers and acres of flourishing green coffee plantations. The state of Andhra Pradesh is called the 'granary of the south' because of the variety of its abundant crops of rice. It is also noted for its chilli crop – this includes the famed pungent red chillies of Guntur.

ABOVE A vibrant array of fruit and vegetables at a market stall in south India.

Kerala is the smallest state in India, and a land of exuberant beauty. There are monsoon-fed rivers, beguiling backwaters and beautiful lagoons. Sandy beaches shimmer with golden sunshine filtering through the palm-fringed coastline.

Fish, shellfish and coconuts are available in abundance, and these ingredients feature in many of the local favourite recipes. Kerala's most prized feature is its fabulous spice plantations. Indeed, the state is often referred to as the 'spice bowl of India'.

LEFT Boats moored on the tranquil palm-fringed backwaters in the beautiful state of Kerala in southern India.

ABOVE The east-Indian district of Darjeeling is famed for its lush tea plantations.

Landscapes of the east

The east-Indian states provide some of the most stunning contrasts of the entire sub-continent. Here, as well as the Ganges plains, you will find the magnificent eastern stretch of the Himalayas which includes Darjeeling with its rolling tea plantations, together with Sikkim and Bhutan with their huge lakes and rivers full of fish. West Bengal is rich in natural resources such as jute, tea, coal and iron, and has a diverse cultural heritage. Rice crops flourish in eastern India, with approximately 30 per cent of the country's total rice crop being produced in this region. Fish is abundantly available in the Bay of Bengal.

Hilly north-east

The north-east of India is a large area with seven states, including Assam and Sikkim, each one keeping its distinctly different cultures and traditions. Rice, tea and turmeric are the main food crops here and the region is also renowned for its exquisite silk. The hill states have their own distinct style of food, with plenty of meat dishes. Many fruits and vegetables are grown and eaten fresh, or dried for use in winter.

The heartland

Central India (Madhya Pradesh) is fondly known as 'the heart of India'. It offers beautiful hill ranges overlooking the Ganges plain, and has fertile black volcanic soil. There is an abundance of wildlife in the dense forests. There is no definitive cuisine style of this area, but it borrows heavily from neighbouring states such as Gujarat, Rajasthan and Bihar.

Western seaboard

The states of Rajasthan, Maharashtra, Gujarat and Goa form western India. The breathtaking variety of landscapes in this region include tidal mudflats, steep ravines, beautiful beaches and coastal lowlands where coconut palms and paddy fields create an incredible view. Wheat, cotton, bananas, sorghum and millet, together with rice, are grown extensively inland; fish and shellfish are the main products in the coastal region. Coconut milk, coconut oil and groundnut oil are produced and used in everyday cooking. The princely state of Rajasthan, an arid land near the borders of Pakistan, gave rise to a sumptuous royal cuisine. Gujarat and Maharashtra are mainly vegetarian, while Goa has a unique style of cuisine – a blend of East and West.

RIGHT The vast land of India spans from neighbouring Afghanistan in the far north to Sri Lanka in the south.

History, religion and festivals

India is a vast country, with a total population of around 1.5 billion. The huge variations in terms of climate, geography and customs have had a powerful influence on the cuisine of India. History and religion have also played their part in the development of cultural and culinary traditions and the shaping of eating habits. The many different influences have helped the country's cooking to emerge as one of the most colourful and exotic in the world.

The influence of immigrants

In the north, nomadic tribes, pilgrims and traders entered India through the Khyber Pass and introduced their particular styles of cooking, which had an enormous impact on Indian cuisine. The mighty Mughals from Persia invaded India through this same mountain pass during the 16th century. The Mughals ruled India for many years and this stability ensured that their elaborate and sophisticated cuisine would become very popular, not only in India, but also outside it. The wide range of cultures that flourished in the northern region gave rise to a rich and tasty fare.

The western side of India came under the influence of the ancient Persians who fled their country to avoid religious persecution. They landed in the province of Gujarat and became known as the 'Parsis'. The contribution of the Parsis to Indian cooking has been invaluable. They combined meat with the traditional vegetarian cuisine of Gujarat to produce rich and uniquely flavoured dishes.

Adventurous Portuguese traders came to India in search of spices and other precious items during the late 15th century and established themselves as traders on the west coast. The Portuguese ruled Goa for four hundred years. During that time, they made significant contributions to the food culture of this region. The influences and tastes they left behind are reflected in the colourful and exotic cuisine of this area.

The eastern belt of India offers a dramatically different range of food. The native cuisine is Bengali which offers a diverse range of dishes, many of them based on fish and rice, with unique flavours. The influence of Tibetan cooking still remains in this region, as well as the unique Anglo-Indian cuisine, a reminder of the British who lived in the area during the early days of the Raj when Calcutta was the capital city.

Southern India offers an inimitable range of food but with very clear regional variations. The beautiful palm-fringed Malabar coast in the south lured foreign powers for centuries, starting with the early Arabians, then the Romans, Chinese, Portuguese and English. These immigrants later spread right across India, and were actively involved in the spice trade.

ABOVE The stunning Taj Mahal mausoleum was built by Mughal Emperor Shah Jahan in memory of his favourite wife.

In Kerala, there are still some Jewish-influenced dishes such as spiced fish, brought by the Jews who came to India from Syria.

Religious influences

India is a land of many religions: Hindu, Muslim, Christian, Sikh, Jain and Buddhist. Religious influence on Indian food has been profound. Hindus and Muslims predominate overall, and they have certain restrictions: for example, Hindus do not eat beef, as the cow is considered to have been the

RIGHT A Hindu woman carries bananas during the Chhath festival celebrations in Kolkata, India. This is one of the most important celebrations in the north-east Indian states of Uttar Pradesh and Bihar.

companion of Lord Krishna, which made it sacred. The holy Koran prohibits Muslims from eating pork or consuming alcohol. The Sikh community's holy scripture, Adi Granth, prohibits them from consuming beef and alcohol. The Sikh, Jain and Buddhist religions have been carved out of the Hindu religion and, therefore, have some food restrictions and customs in common with Hinduism. However, these religions also display many distinctive features of their own.

In the Hindu religion, each of the gods and goddesses are worshipped as the patron of a particular profession or trade. For example, a farmer would naturally worship the Sun God and the God of Rain. Each god is believed to have his particular favourite dish which the farmer would make as an offering so that the god blesses him with a fruitful harvest.

Festival food

The sheer number of different religious affiliations in India has given rise to a huge variety of special foods and recipes. Festivals are very important – there are 13 major festivals in every year. Each of these celebrations belongs to a different religion, and each has its own distinct style of food, with religious traditions dictating what is to be cooked and served. However, it is not just the religious aspect that determines celebratory cuisine: festivals are also associated with the season and the crops that are growing or have just been harvested.

Muslims observe a month-long fast during Ramadan, after which comes the festival of Id-al-Fitr. The celebration table in India includes such delicacies as pilaus, biryanis, all kinds of kebabs and speciality breads.

Diwali, referred to internationally as the Festival of Lights, is a major religious celebration which is marked throughout India by Hindus, Jains and Sikhs. During the Diwali festival, sweets and fruit are distributed among family and friends in order to celebrate the victory of good over evil and light over darkness. Fireworks are set off to light up the night sky during this joyful celebration.

RIGHT Young women carry oil lamps on the eve of Diwali, the Hindu Festival of Lights. Hindus around the world light lamps during Diwali to symbolize the victory of good over evil.

Regional cooking

Through the centuries, each state of India has developed its own unique signature dishes and distinct styles of cooking. From the clay-oven-baked tandooris of the north to the coconut-fuelled dishes of the south, cooking styles and recipes are heavily influenced by the diversity of climate and geography, which greatly determines the choice of ingredients available. Nevertheless, there are often similarities such as the use of cardamom pods, cumin, coriander, ginger and fiery chillies.

ABOVE A baker in Mumbai proudly shows off a tray piled high with freshly prepared naan, which is a popular accompaniment to many Indian meals.

Rural cuisine

Across rural India, where transport and communication are not as efficient as they are in urban areas, people rely heavily on locally grown produce. In general, lentils, peas and fresh vegetables are very important to an Indian family. These are cooked and served on a daily basis with small helpings of meat, poultry or fish. Chapatis or other bread products provide plenty of dietary fibre, while rice is essential for the required daily amount of carbohydrates, giving plenty of energy for an outdoor life based on farming or fishing.

City life

The main cities of India are set far apart – Delhi in the north, Kolkata (formerly Calcutta) in the far east, Chennai (Madras) on the south-eastern seaboard and Mumbai (formerly Bombay) on the west coast. These busy centres with their thronging populations developed their own cuisines, with local delicacies such as Alur Chop, the tasty little meat and potato patties created in Kolkata a century or two ago and now found on every street corner. Cities such as Jaipur and Udaipur in Rajasthan (the abode of kings) boast delectable game recipes which originated in royal kitchens. The kings and princes would return from hunting laden with game, which their chefs turned into deliciously rich dishes such as Stuffed Quails (Batair Mussallam).

The chapati is the most commonly eaten basic bread throughout the whole country; it is indispensable to an Indian family. Breads are made from rice flour (chawal ki roti) and maize flour (makki ki roti) as well as wheat. In more affluent families, fancy breads, such as parathas, naans and puris are more popular.

Traditions of the north

In the remote mountainous areas all along the north and the north-east borders of India, cooking is restricted to what grows naturally in the area and what the farmers can produce and preserve themselves. The staples in the far north consist mainly of rice, millet, maize and potatoes. These are eaten with vegetables for a balanced diet. In some northern areas people cook or smoke locally reared meat over wood fires. Tea plantations are everywhere, and the distinctive smoky taste of Assam tea from this area is renowned the world over.

Away from the remote border regions, the food of northern India is more diverse. Staples include wheat and rice as well as roti, meaning bread, which is generally made from grains, salt and water. In rural areas, people grind their own wheat, using traditional hand utensils and techniques, to make flour, and their bread is made with just the ground wheat, water and salt, baked on a cast iron griddle.

In the capital city of Delhi, there are spicy tandoori delicacies alongside an exquisite, rich Mughlai cuisine with its silky smooth sauces, fragrant biryanis and pilaus. The city of Lucknow in Uttar Pradesh, in the provinces bordering remote Nepal, has developed its own style of cuisine known as Awadhi that is a reminder of the luxury of the bygone times of maharajahs and princes. Kashmir, the beautiful northernmost state, has yet another unique cuisine based on locally grown fruits and nuts which are added to recipes to produce a variety of sumptuous meat and poultry dishes. Kashmiri cuisine is prized for its unusual richness and varied textures and flavours, and dishes such as kormas, pasandas and biryanis are now firmly established as some of the most popular foods of the north.

The technique of blending and cooking with spices has developed in different ways throughout India. In the state of Punjab, for example, spices are used to marinate meat, fish and vegetables for its renowned tandoori cooking. When a dish is cooked in a clay oven fuelled by charcoal, the spice-laced food has a completely different taste from the same ingredients cooked in an ordinary oven. It is also a very healthy way of cooking, as it preserves all the nutrients within the covered dish.

Another legendary tradition is the Kashmiri banquet known as *wazawaan*. The banquet is named after special chefs who are known as *wazas*; they use generous amounts of aromatic spices such as aniseed, cinnamon and cardamom.

ABOVE Herbs and spices are abundantly available at street markets across India.

Eastern flavours

In rural east India, people have developed their own culinary styles using locally grown fresh ginger, turmeric, mustard and sweet peppers. Dairy products, fresh mangoes and coconuts are grown in abundance, and there are numerous varieties of fish from the rivers and the sea. Bengali cuisine uses an extensive range of spices and one of the typical flavours of this region is the wonderfully fragrant panchforon, consisting of five types of seeds: black mustard, cumin, nigella (kalonji), fennel and fenugreek. Again, rice is the staple dish on which all dishes are based. Many of the favourite recipes of this area are characterized by the distinctive, pungent flavour of mustard oil.

One of the most fascinating features of Bengal is Mog cuisine. This style of cooking is named after a Buddhist tribe whose

BELOW A Kashmiri cook pounds mutton to make haleem for a banquet or *wazawaan*.

BELOW Fresh, hand-picked chillies are laid out in the sun to dry.

BELOW Women transporting baskets of fish from boats in the eastern state of Orissa.

origins are found in the hilly parts of Bangladesh, in the far north-east. The Mog cooks were skilled in creating a range of dishes based on the principles of 'East Meets West'. These dishes were great favourites among the British living in the state of Assam, where they were engaged in growing tea. When India gained independence in 1947 and the British departed, the talented Mog cooks found employment within Indian families.

The diverse west

Western India, especially the state of Gujarat, is well known for its dairy produce. It plays an important part in the daily diet, which is mainly vegetarian. The generous Gujarati thali (large platter) meals are famous throughout the country. Rajasthan, north of Gujarat, has many vegetarians, and the food of this region has a unique richness and flavour due to the use of pure butterfat ghee (clarified butter). As well as making a variety of cooked dishes using dairy foods, the people of Rajasthan and Gujarat also consume a lot of yogurt and buttermilk on a daily basis.

BELOW In many rural locations chapatis are still made over an open fire.

Root vegetables, lentils and groundnut oil are produced in the west and used in everyday cooking, and mangoes, coconuts and cashew nuts also grow in profusion. Here in the west of India, a vast patchwork of paddy fields with their raised borders and swaying coconut palm trees makes a memorable sight. Along the coastline there is plenty of fish and shellfish, and this, combined with rice, forms the basis of the daily diet of the coastal population.

Maharashtra, a large province along the shores of the Arabian Sea, has its own cuisine, except in the capital city of Mumbai (Bombay), which is a kaleidoscope of food cultures because of its mixed population. Farther down to the south of Mumbai is the tiny state of Goa, popularly known as Golden Goa or the Pearl of the Orient. Goa has a food tradition which is formed by a rich tapestry of historical influences, a blend of East and West, owing to its colonization by the Portuguese five centuries ago. This is where the famous vindaloo originated – a dish well known for its fieriness, but which should in fact be well balanced in spiciness. Goa is particularly renowned for its vast range of different fish and shellfish dishes, such as jhinga caldeen, a delicious mixture of prawns (shrimp), spices and creamed coconut. The flesh of coconuts and vinegar made of coconut sap give Goan cuisine its distinctive flavour, and are used in daily cooking to produce delicious sweet and savoury dishes.

Coconut feni, a very potent liquor made from the sap of the coconut palm tree, is the most popular drink in Goa.

The hot south

The southern Indian economy thrives on spices and rice, as well as coconut and its by-products. South India is one of the leading exporters of prime quality spices and the international trade in spices, which started many centuries ago, has enjoyed phenomenal growth in recent years. This is also the land of tea and coffee plantations, as well as the golden harvest of rice. A huge industry has grown up based around

ABOVE Traditional techniques for grinding grain can still be observed in rural India.

coconut – as well as cooking with the flesh and milk, coconut oil is used all over southern India; the outer shell is cleaned and polished to make bowls, and other parts of the plant are used to make such essentials as roofs and pillars for rural huts. In more far-flung country areas, the outer hairy coir is used as a cooking fuel.

In the south-east, the state of Andhra Pradesh has developed its own distinctive cuisine which sets it apart from other southern states. Because of the Muslim influence, Andhra Pradesh has more meat eaters than vegetarians. Mughlai cuisine thrives in the city of Hyderabad, where the last Mughal emperor made his home. It is a way of cooking that uses many rich ingredients such as cream, meat, spices, fruit and nuts to make sumptuous dishes for special occasions.

Chilli peppers grow abundantly in the south, so the food tends to be quite fiery. On the other hand, the cuisine of Kerala evolved around the abundance of locally available salty seafood and soothing coconut, rather similar to the classic dishes of Goa farther up the coast.

Classic ingredients

Certain ingredients are vital to Indian cooking, but apart from a handful that are used throughout the country, these foodstuffs vary a great deal from one region to another. Even among the few common items, such as onion, ginger, garlic, bread and rice, the methods of preparation and cooking may vary, which results in very different flavours. Indians believe that food is a gift of nature, and that harmony of body, mind and soul must be created through a balance of food types.

Spices and other flavourings

To Indian cooks, spices are the blood in their veins; without them Indian food would be like the summer sky without the sun.

Aniseed This has a delicate liquorice flavour and sweet seeds. It makes a good aid to digestion.

Asafoetida This spice has a powerful aroma and is often used in cooking pulses. It is added to hot oil which mellows its strong smell and complements the dish.

Cardamom, cinnamon and cloves These three sweetish spices have been an integral part of Indian cooking since ancient times. Cardamom is native to India where it is considered to be the most prized spice after saffron. The pods can be used whole or the husks can be removed to release the seeds, and they have a slightly pungent but very aromatic taste. South Indians use ground cardamom in their desserts and sweetmeats while northerners are passionate about its sweet, heady aroma in chicken dishes, pilaus and biryanis. The three spices are used to make a spicy infusion in the north, as these ingredients are known to raise body temperature and are ideal to fight the cold winter climate.

Chillies It is surprising that chillies, without which Indian food is difficult to imagine, were not known in India until the 16th century when the Portuguese introduced them to the southern region. South Indians are probably the biggest consumers of chillies; their food is renowned for its pungency. The state of Andhra Pradesh is the biggest producer, and many exotic dishes using chillies originated here. Dried red chillies and chilli powder are used widely all over India.

Coriander (cilantro) and cumin These two spices are used in almost every savoury dish cooked in India. Dried coriander has a sweet, mellow flavour, and cumin is its traditional companion. In north India zeera aloo (cumin potatoes) has cumin as the main flavouring; korma recipes, on the other hand, are flavoured with generous quantities of coriander but with little cumin. Other well-known dishes such as jhalfrazi and do piaza have equal quantities of each spice.

BELOW Cloves add an enticing flavour to many dishes – both sweet and savoury.

BELOW Fresh, dried and powdered chillies spice up cuisine throughout India.

BELOW In India pickles are a popular accompaniment to many main dishes.

ABOVE The smaller a garlic bulb the more potent its flavour tends to be.

ABOVE Spices and flavourings play an essential role in all Indian cooking.

ABOVE Saffron is an expensive spice but only a tiny amount is needed per recipe.

Ginger, onion and garlic These three ingredients are often the key elements in Indian food. Garlic is a standard ingredient, along with ginger, in most curries. It can be used pulped, crushed or chopped. Whole cloves are sometimes added to dishes. Ginger is one of India's oldest and most popular spices. In the north, onion, ginger and garlic are often used as an all-in-one paste, or onions are boiled and puréed before being cooked with ginger, garlic and dry spices. Browned onion purée is another way of creating a distinctive flavour.

Nigella This aromatic spice has a sharp and tingling taste and is used mainly to add flavour to vegetable dishes.

Garam masala There is no set recipe for this mixture of spices, but a typical mixture might include peppercorns, black cumin seeds, cloves, cinnamon and black cardamom pods.

Star anise This is a star-shaped, liquorice-flavoured pod.

Herbs Indian housewives will not consider sending a dish to the dining table without a handful of fresh coriander (cilantro). The leaves of this fragrant and pretty plant are used to garnish almost every savoury dish. Curry leaves also play an important part in south Indian cooking. They are to south Indian cooking what fresh coriander and garam masala are to the north. The leaves of the fenugreek plant, together with its seeds, are often used, for example in the famous north Indian dish methi gosht (lamb with fenugreek).

Mustard seeds These are another essential ingredient in Indian cooking, especially in vegetarian dishes. In the south, jet-black mustard seeds adorn snow-white home-made yogurt as a dressing for all kinds of salads. On the other hand, the creamy-yellow variety of mustard seed is used to make certain curries as well as the majority of pickles.

Fennel seeds These are very similar in appearance to cumin seeds, have a very sweet taste and are used to flavour certain curries. Fennel seeds can also be chewed as a mouth-freshener after a spicy meal.

Fenugreek This fresh herb has very small leaves and is sold in bunches. It is used to flavour meat and vegetarian dishes. The stalks should be discarded as they will impart a bitterness to a dish if used. Fenugreek seeds are flat in appearance, extremely pungent and slightly bitter.

Nutmeg and mace The nutmeg plant is unique in that it produces two spices in one: nutmeg (jaiphal) and mace (javitri). These are both highly aromatic spices and are used extensively in northern cuisine. Ground mace, along with cardamom, gives a distinctive flavour to poultry dishes which are cooked in the *tandoor*, a type of clay oven.

Saffron This is used in both sweet and savoury dishes, and is known to have medicinal values such as curing skin and stomach disorders. The stigmas of the saffron crocus flower are hand picked and sun-dried, and they are so light that it takes about 500,000 dried stigmas to make 450g (1lb) of saffron. A few strands soaked in a little milk or water will add an exotic taste and appearance to any dish.

Turmeric The rich golden hue of turmeric has a bitter taste that disappears when blended with other ingredients. Turmeric is highly antiseptic, with exceptional preserving qualities. Fish is often sprinkled with turmeric and salt if it cannot be cooked on the same day as it is bought.

Other flavourings

Sweet, sour, salty, pungent and bitter tastes are all important in Indian cooking.

ABOVE Fresh, sour tamarind is cooked with rice, fish and meat to add seasoning.

ABOVE Many Indian recipes traditionally use ghee to cook with.

ABOVE Recipes rich in coconut are a hallmark of south Indian cuisine.

Palm sugar (jaggery) is traditionally used for a sweet taste. There are several souring agents, but the most commonly used ones are tamarind and dried mango powder. They each impart their own distinctive taste and flavour to a dish.

Dry mango powder Mangoes are indigenous to India, and they have many uses in Indian cooking. The fruit is used in curries at different stages of ripeness, but the unripe fruit is also sun-dried and ground into a dry powder called amchur. The powder has a sour taste, and is sprinkled over dishes as a garnish; it is not used in cooking.

Mustard seed oil Made from mustard seeds, this oil has a pungent taste when raw but becomes sweeter when heated.

Tamarind Dried black tamarind pods are sour in taste and very sticky. Tamarind can be bought in paste, but lemon juice can be used as a substitute.

Rice

As the main source of carbohydrate in the Indian diet, rice accompanies almost every Indian meal. However, it is not just eaten as a savoury dish. Throughout the country rice pudding with nuts, cardamom and saffron is a holy offering which is also cooked as a dessert. Delicately flavoured basmati rice is India's most popular type of rice.

Dairy products

Yogurt, buttermilk and cheese are very important ingredients in India; they provide protein for the majority of the population who are vegetarians. Plain yogurt accompanies most Indian meals, and drinks based on yogurt are also very popular. Punjabi lassi is enjoyed all over India, and buttermilk is used in cooking as well as for a refreshing drink. Paneer, the only Indian cheese, is an important ingredient for both sweet and savoury dishes. North India's signature dish, matter paneer, is a delicious blend of paneer and peas in a richly spiced tomato sauce.

Oil and butter

Sunflower oil is the most popular cooking medium because of its neutral flavour, but in some regions cooks favour groundnut oil or mustard oil. Rich, nutty-tasting clarified butter (ghee) was the traditional medium of cooking until recent years. It is made by gently heating unsalted (sweet) butter until all the moisture evaporates and the milk solids settle. It can then be strained and stored at room temperature.

Vegetables and fruit

In a nation that is mainly vegetarian, vegetables and fruit have an important nutritional role to play, as well as imparting their distinctive tastes to most dishes.

Aubergines (eggplants) These have been used in India for more than 4,000 years. Each region has its own way of preparing and cooking aubergines, for instance bharta (mashed and spiced) in the north and vangi bhat (spiced aubergine rice) in the west.

Beans These are among the most popular vegetables. Both French beans and runner beans are used in spicy stir-fries, or cooked with lentils, or steamed and seasoned with whole spices to make salads.

Tomatoes The tomatoes that are widely grown and used in Indian cooking resemble Italian plum tomatoes. Chopped tomatoes, mixed with onion, green chilli and coriander (cilantro) leaves, make a popular salad.

Coconut This popular ingredient is used all over the country, but especially in the south, to flavour sweet and savoury dishes. It is regularly used to make coconut desserts and sweetmeats for festivals. Fresh coconut can usually be substituted with desiccated (dry unsweetened shredded) or coconut cream.

ABOVE The national fruit of India, juicy mangoes are grown throughout the land.

Mango During the short mango season, plump, juicy mangoes adorn the market stalls. Ripe fresh mangoes are used in sweet dishes; green or unripe mangoes can be used in curries and to make mango chutney.

Pineapple Grown mainly in the south and the north-east, pineapples are cooked with spices to make palate-cleansing side dishes.

Beans, peas and lentils

A good source of protein and fibre, beans, peas and lentils are cooked with meat or vegetables and are used in soups and dhals.

Chana dhal This round split yellow lentil is used as a binding agent in some dishes.

Masoor dhal These split red lentils are actually orange in colour and turn a pale yellow when cooked. Whole brown lentils are a type of red lentil with the husk intact.

Toor dhal A shiny split lentil, toor dhal is similar in size to chana dhal.

Chickpeas These round, beige-coloured pulses have a strong, nutty flavour when cooked. They are used in curries, ground into a flour that is used in many dishes, such as pakoras and bhajiyas, and are also added to Indian snacks.

ABOVE Protein-rich nuts are a popular addition to sweet and savoury dishes.

Mung beans These small round green beans are sweet with a creamy texture. When sprouted, mung beans produce beansprouts. Split mung beans are also used, and are often cooked with rice.

Nuts and seeds

The delicious flavour of many nuts adds an extra dimension and great nutritional value to many recipes, both sweet and savoury.

Almonds These nuts are used in making rich sauces, especially kormas and pasandas. They grow in abundance in Kashmir in the north where, a superb chutney is made from ground blanched almonds and spices.

Cashew nuts These full-flavoured nuts are an important ingredient in Indian cooking. In the north they are soaked and ground to a purée to make thick, rich sauces. In Goa, a powerful liquor called kaju feni is made from the sap of the cashew plant.

Pistachio nuts These sweet, green nuts are used mainly in desserts and sweets. Raw or toasted pistachio nuts make attractive garnishes for pilaus and biryanis. Pista burfi, a fudge-like sweetmeat, is very popular.

Walnuts These are commonly used in sweetmeats, salads and raitas.

ABOVE Indian coastal waters provide a rich and varied source of seafood.

Sesame seeds These small, flat pear-shaped seeds are usually white but can be cream, brown, red or black. When roasted or dry-fried they take on a slightly nutty taste.

Pomegranate seeds These can be extracted from fresh pomegranates or bought in jars. The seeds impart a delicious tangy flavour.

Meat

Chicken is the most popular meat in India, and it is also the most expensive. No banquet or special occasion meal is cooked without one or two chicken dishes on the menu. Beef and pork are less commonly eaten as the cow is sacred to Hindus and the Koran prohibits Muslims from eating pork. Lamb is not commonly used, apart from in the Himalayas; instead mutton and goat are more popular.

Fish and shellfish

Almost two-thirds of India is surrounded by sea and the fish found in these waters, such as mackerel, sardine, tuna and monkfish, form the basis of an amazing range of recipes. Most of these fish lend themselves well to curries. Among the shellfish, prawns (shrimp) are the most popular, and mussels, crabs and lobsters are cooked in spicy coconut broth all along the southern coastal regions.

Tools and equipment

Throughout India, using the appropriate equipment, together with different cooking techniques, helps to produce the flavours, colours and textures that are characteristic to each dish. Most of the cooking is done in heavy cast iron, steel or copper cooking pots and pans which help to distribute the heat evenly. They also allow the food to cook without losing any of the natural moisture and enable spices to be pre-fried without sticking to the bottom of the pan.

Cooking utensils

There is a vast array of favourite cooking utensils in India. All along the coastal regions of southern India, terracotta cooking pots are preferred. These are generally unglazed as aeration is easier, and this means that the food does not need immediate refrigeration in spite of the extreme heat in the south. In the north, the emphasis is more on sealing cooking pots well so that the flavour of the food is concentrated inside – a method of cooking known as dum.

Handi This cooking pot is used to make many dum dishes. It is traditionally a copper pot with a neck which is narrower than the base, rather like a bigger version of a *degchi*. Decorated ovenproof *handis* made from terracotta are now commonly available and have become a favourite in the modern kitchen.

Kadhai/karahi Fried puffed breads (puri and luchi) are deep-fried in a round-bottomed pan, similar to a wok, known as a *kadhai* or *karahi*. A *kadhai* is also needed for all types of bhuna (stir-fried) dishes, and an amazing range of mouthwatering dishes have been created based on this humble cooking utensil. All over north India and the north-west frontier (now in Pakistan) such dishes as bhuna gosht (goat or lamb cooked by the stir-frying method), kadhai murgh (chicken) and kadhai paneer (Indian cheese) are very popular. The *kadhai* is probably one of the oldest cooking utensils in India – archaeologists have discovered the ancient remains of a pan that closely resembles the *kadhai*. Today this pan is a common sight in every domestic and restaurant kitchen and every street-side eatery in north India and Pakistan.

Patila A heavy steel pan with a lid, known as a *patila*, is used for making stocks, kormas and bhuna dishes. Kormas need heavy cooking pots with tight-fitting lids as very little liquid is used during the cooking process in order to encourage the meat or poultry to cook in their own delicious juices. Korma, which means braising, is essentially a technique of cooking rather than a particular dish.

BELOW The *handi* cooking pot, which is traditionally made out of copper, has a narrower neck than the base.

BELOW The round-bottomed, wok-like *kadhai* is used to make deep-fried puffed bread and bhuna (stir-fried) dishes.

BELOW A *patila* is a heavy steel pan with a lid which is commonly used for making stocks and kormas.

ABOVE Traditional Indian metal cooking pots are now also available in terracotta.

Lagan In Lucknow, northern India, a shallow copper utensil known as a *lagan* is used for cooking large cuts of meat such as lamb shanks or chops and whole chickens. The *lagan* has a slightly rounded bottom and a heavy, tight-fitting lid, which also makes it ideal for dum dishes, especially in this part of northern India, where the traditional method of using both direct and indirect heat is used. The temperature for dum cooking needs to be quite gentle, so when the prepared food is put on dum the heat is turned down very low, and indirect heat is created by placing live charcoal on the lid. The lid of a *lagan* is known as a *seeni*. This method can be replicated in the Western world by cooking the dish in a low oven, as long as the pot is sealed well.

Degchi Pilau and biryani dishes require a specially shaped pot called a *degchi* which is capable of generating steam from within. The food is cooked entirely in the steam, which produces succulent and well-flavoured meat or poultry and slender, dry grains of rice. The *degchi*, which is traditionally made of either brass or copper, is pear-shaped, with a narrow neck to help to keep all the steam inside, so the food can breathe as it cooks. This cooking technique is known as dum. A sticky dough made of flour is used all around the neck of the pot in order to hold the lid in place and to ensure that no steam can escape. North India has mastered the art of dum cooking, and tasty, tender dishes such as dum machchi, dum aloo, and all types of biryanis have tantalized the taste buds of the nation as well as visitors to India.

It is, however, possible to cook biryanis and other dum dishes successfully in a standard cooking pot as long as it is made of heavy steel or copper. To replicate the sealing process of the *degchi*, well-moistened baking parchment can be used to cover the top layer of rice, which should again be covered with a moist tea towel. A double thickness of foil added before putting the lid on will seal the pan well and allow the biryani to cook to perfection.

Tawa Chapati, everyone's daily bread in India, is cooked on a cast iron griddle known as a *tawa*, which is also used for cooking the majority of the unleavened flat breads. A bigger and heavier version of the domestic *tawa* is used by the street vendors in India. The street *tawas* are used to produce the most delicious snacks, the aromas of which fill the air, drawing people towards the *tawa* like a magnet.

BELOW The *tawa* is a flat hot griddle pan traditionally used to cook chapatis on.

Chapati rolling board This round wooden board on short stubby legs is used to mould breads into shape.

Chapati spoon The square, flat-headed chapati spoon is used for turning roasting breads on the hot chapati griddle. A fish slice (spatula) may also be used.

Tandoor Leavened breads such as naans of various kinds are cooked in a *tandoor*, a barrel-shaped clay oven. It is believed to have found its way into India from Egypt, where it is known as a *tanoor*. The *tandoor* was originally used only for making naan. History has it that the practice was started in Egypt during the construction of the great pyramids. Because of the vast demand for food for the workers, especially bread, the Egyptians used the same kind of stones that were being used to construct the pyramids to make a grinding stone for wheat, which was then mixed with water to make bread, and baked in the *tanoor*. Thus the tradition of baking was born. It found its way into Persia, to Afghanistan, then finally to northern India. Punjabi tandoor cooking is celebrated all over India, while tandoori chicken and chicken tikka have established themselves as firm favourites all over the world.

BELOW The chapati rolling pin is available in many different sizes.

Tapeli Used for cooking rice, a *tapeli* is a useful pan made of heavy stainless steel or copper. A *tapeli* is shaped like a normal pan, but has a tight-fitting lid which is ideal for cooking rice by the absorption method.

Slotted spoon Stirring cooked, drained rice with a slotted spoon will make the rice soft and fluffy by allowing air in between the grains. The slotted spoon is also useful for removing food from hot oils and liquids.

Cooking with spices

In an ideal world, freshly ground spices are the only way to achieve full flavours, but modern day life is stressful enough and it is difficult to find the time to cook a meal from scratch, let alone time to grind the spices! In India, domestic help is quite readily available, and kitchen staff may be able to assist in preparing freshly ground spices. Ready-ground spices can be used instead, with care and if time is short.

Traditional methods Whole spices have a longer shelf life than pre-ground and can be ground in small quantities as and when required. Some Indian households still use the traditional grinding stone known as a *sil-batta*, which is made up of two pieces. One of the stones is a flat platform on which the spices are placed and the other, a small cylindrical roller, is used to grind the spices into a wet spice paste. This method produces fabulous flavours but is time-consuming so a mortar and pestle, or *haman-dasta*, is more commonly used.

BELOW A mortar and pestle is ideal for grinding up small amounts of fresh spices.

Electric grinders It is worth buying a coffee grinder to keep solely for spice grinding, as the aroma of freshly ground spices is unmatchable. Coffee grinders work well for small quantities of dry ingredients. Traditional grinding stones may make the best chutneys and spice pastes from wet ingredients, but a food processor is the answer for today's busy cooks. It can be used to chop and slice onions and make ginger and garlic purées, which are essential ingredients in Indian cooking.

Using pre-ground spices When stored correctly, pre-ground spices can add perfectly good flavours to cooking, but they have a limited shelf life. Once the spices are ground the essential oils within them start to dry out quite rapidly. It is these oils that impart flavours to the food, so to retain them, buy spices in small quantities and store in air-tight containers away from direct light. Another good way to enhance the flavours of spices is to heat them gently.

BELOW No Indian kitchen would be complete without a box full of spices.

ABOVE The *tadka*, a small wok-like utensil, is used for warming oils and spices.

Spice box A *masala dani*, or spice box, is the pride and joy of any Indian housewife. The box is traditionally handed down within a family from mother to daughter or sometimes even grandmother to granddaughter. Spice boxes are available in all manner of shapes, colours and sizes. The most common type contains small steel, cup-like containers which are neatly arranged inside a large box with a lid. The small containers are used for storing the whole spices that are added to everyday dishes. Popular spices include mustard, cumin and nigella seeds, dried red chillies, black peppercorns, and many more. These spices are generally used to flavour pulses and vegetables.

Tadka A small, heavy pan shaped like a miniature wok is used to heat a little oil. A choice of whole spices from the spice box are then thrown into the pan, where they release their amazing aroma. The oil and the whole spices are then folded into the cooked dish. This technique is known as *tadka*, meaning 'seasoning'. In a Western kitchen a steel ladle that can be held over a flame on a gas stove is a perfect substitute for the small heavy pan used in India for preparing hot oil seasonings.

north india

From hearty noodle soups and crispy corn fritters to marinated fish, succulent meat dishes and refreshing iced kulfi, the distinctively aromatic tastes of north India are captured in the following mouthwatering dishes with a delicious difference.

North India

The Himalayas dominate the states of north India, from Kashmir in the north-west to Uttar Pradesh in the south-east of the region. This majestic mountain range stretches from the western border with Pakistan and Afghanistan, right across the northern part of India and Nepal where it borders China, to the far north-eastern states. All of the 14 highest peaks in the world can be found here, including of course Mount Everest. It is no wonder that the food in the northern region is very different from that of the hot, ocean-bathed south. Main dishes often use lamb, goat, chicken, or delicate river fish such as rainbow trout from the rivers that tumble down from the mountains.

But it is not just the climate that makes the difference in north India. Invaders, pilgrims and traders from the north beyond the mountains made their way across the Himalayas centuries ago, aiming to subdue and rule the native people and to make use of their agricultural land. They naturally brought some of their own traditions of farming and cooking with them. For example, the mighty Mughal lords rode through the Khyber Pass in 1526 and imposed their rule on almost the whole of India for 200 years. Their legacy is the popular tradition of Mughal cuisine with its silky smooth sauces and the fragrance of saffron.

In Kashmir, the northernmost state of India, the brightly dressed women tend floating gardens full of vegetables and fruit that flourish around the lakes in the pleasant warmth of summer. In the autumn, fruit trees are laden with plums, peaches, cherries, almonds and walnuts. One important ingredient grown in Kashmir is saffron – the crocus flower from which it is produced grows in large quantities in the cool northern fields. The rich supply of good quality ingredients leads to all sorts of splendid traditions, including that of the Kashmiri banquet. These enormous feasts consist of many courses, each served on large platters shared among the entire community.

Himachal Pradesh, just south of Kashmir, is a mosaic of thick forests, snow-clad peaks and lush, soft green valleys. Spiky pines and verdant, broad-leafed trees cling to the lower slopes of the mountains, while meandering rivers and serene lakes create a beautiful panorama. Agriculture is the main source of income in the state and wheat, maize, barley and rice are grown in abundance where the terrain flattens out below the Himalayan foothills. Farther south again, the Punjab and Uttar Pradesh lie nearer to the hotter central plains of India. Agriculture is the driving force of the economy and fields of corn, wheat and maize flourish everywhere.

The main focus of north Indian food is on bread rather than rice, although Uttar Pradesh produces some of the best basmati rice in India. Lamb and chicken is usually served with a large pot of spicy vegetables, including mustard greens, corn, spinach and tomatoes, and split peas or lentils. North Indians also love dairy products, such as milk, ghee (clarified butter), paneer (Indian cheese) and yogurt. These supply much of the protein in the diet and feature in the many delicious desserts such as Kulfi, a sweet frozen mixture of milk, cream, sugar and nuts.

Noodle Soup with Minced Meat and Vegetables

Thukpa

From the Himalayan region, this hearty soup makes an all-in-one meal, perfect for chilly winter days. Serve as a main dish with hot, crusty bread, or in smaller portions as a tasty first course.

Serves 4

2 tbsp sunflower oil or olive oil
1 large onion, finely chopped
500g/1¼lb/2 cups lean minced (ground) pork, beef or chicken
5cm/2in piece fresh root ginger, grated
4 cloves garlic, finely chopped
2–3 green chillies, finely chopped (and seeded if preferred)
2 vegetable stock (bouillon) cubes
115g/4oz/¾ cup carrots, diced
115g/4oz/¾ cup green beans, cut into 1cm/½in pieces
1 tbsp chopped coriander (cilantro)
salt and pepper to taste
1 fresh red chilli, seeded and cut into julienne strips, to garnish
300g/11oz/2½ cups egg noodles, to serve

1 Heat the oil in a wok over a medium heat and add the onion. Fry for about 8–9 minutes or until the onion turns a golden brown, stirring regularly.

2 Add the minced pork, ginger, garlic and green chillies. Increase the heat to high and cook for 10–12 minutes, stirring regularly.

3 Pour in 2 litres/3½ pints/8 cups warm water and add the stock cubes. Bring to the boil and stir until the stock cubes are dissolved. Add the carrots and cook for 5 minutes.

4 Add the green beans and salt to taste. Cook for 5–6 minutes longer, then sprinkle in the chopped coriander and stir. Remove the wok from the heat.

5 To serve, boil the noodles according to the instructions on the packet, then drain and rinse them well in cold water. Season the noodles with salt and pepper and add 1 tbsp olive oil to prevent them sticking. Place the noodles in serving bowls, then top with the soup and serve garnished with the red chilli strips.

Variation

In the Himalayas, yak meat is widely used but minced (ground) pork, beef or chicken can be substituted.

PER PORTION Energy 614kcal/2579kJ; Protein 38.4g; Carbohydrate 64.8g, of which sugars 9.7g; Fat 24.2g, of which saturates 7.7g; Cholesterol 92.5mg; Calcium 75.5mg; Fibre 4.85g; Sodium 362.5mg.

Serves 8

175g/6oz/1½ cups gram flour
pinch of bicarbonate of soda (baking soda)
1 tsp salt or to taste
1 tsp crushed dried red chillies
1 tsp nigella seeds
½ tsp fennel seeds
½ tsp cumin seeds
½ tsp ground turmeric
1 tsp ground cumin
200ml/7fl oz/¾ cup water
225g/8oz/1⅓ cups whole baby corn
sunflower oil or olive oil for deep-frying
chutney, to serve (optional)

PER PORTION Energy 222kcal/928kJ; Protein 6g; Carbohydrate 22.3g, of which sugars 1.1g; Fat 12.9g, of which saturates 1.6g; Cholesterol 0mg; Calcium 29mg; Fibre 3.2g; Sodium 431mg.

Baby Corn Fritters

Makki ke Pakore

Corn is grown extensively in the state of Punjab and is used in many different ways in Punjabi cooking. Made from tender whole baby corn, these delicious fritters are simple to make and can accompany a wide selection of dishes. With their tangy bite of distinctly Indian spices and chillies, they also make a mouthwatering snack to serve with afternoon drinks.

1 In a medium-sized mixing bowl, mix all the dry ingredients together and gradually add the water to form a thick paste of a consistency that will stick to the corn.

2 Heat the oil over a medium heat in a wok or other suitable pan for deep-frying. When the surface of the oil takes on a faint shimmer of rising smoke, dip each baby corn into the batter and shake off any excess mixture.

3 Fry the corn fritters in a single layer, without overcrowding them in the pan, until they are crisp and golden brown, or about 7–8 minutes.

4 Drain the corn fritters on absorbent kitchen paper. Serve with mango or other chutney if you wish, although they are delicious enough to eat on their own. They taste especially good with cold beer or a chilled white wine.

Serves 4

675g/1½lb fillet of cod, haddock or other white fish
2 shallots, roughly chopped
25g/1oz/2 tbsp fresh root ginger, roughly chopped
2–4 green chillies, roughly chopped and seeded if preferred
15g/½oz/¼ cup coriander (cilantro) leaves and stalks, roughly chopped
1 tbsp tamarind juice or 2 tbsp lemon juice
1 tsp salt, or to taste
75g/3oz/⅔ cup gram flour, sifted
oil for deep-frying

Variation

Serve with chunky chips (French fries) for a meal of 'fish and chips', Indian style.

PER PORTION Energy 356.8kcal/1490kJ; Protein 35g; Carbohydrate 13.6g, of which sugars 1.6g; Fat 18.3g, of which saturates 2.2g; Cholesterol 80.5mg; Calcium 55.8mg; Fibre 2.6g; Sodium 116.2mg.

Fillets of Fish Coated in Green Spice Paste

Hara Masale ki Machchi

A delicious paste of fresh coriander, lemon juice, root ginger, garlic and chilli is used to marinate the fish in this recipe, creating a refreshing taste. Any white fish may be used here – even flaky fish – as it is coated with gram flour before frying.

1 Wash the fish gently under running water and pat dry with absorbent kitchen paper. Cut into 5cm/2in pieces. Put the fish in a large mixing bowl.

2 Process the shallots, ginger, chillies, coriander, tamarind or lemon juice and salt in a food processor or liquidizer (blender). If you are using a liquidizer, add 2–3 tbsp water to ensure that the blade does not stick. Add the blended ingredients to the fish, and using a metal spoon, mix gently, but thoroughly. Set aside for about 30 minutes.

3 Add the sifted gram flour and 2–3 tbsp water, if necessary, and mix thoroughly until the fish is coated with the paste. You can add a little more water if the paste is not wet enough, to ensure the fish are coated thoroughly.

4 Heat the oil in a wok or other suitable pan for deep-frying over a medium to high heat, then fry the fish in batches for 2½ minutes on each side until they are a golden brown colour. Drain the fried fish on absorbent kitchen paper and serve with any vegetable or lentil dish, accompanied by plain boiled rice.

Rainbow Trout in Lemon and Mustard Marinade

Kullu Trout

In this recipe, whole trout are marinated in a mixture of mustard oil, chilli, lemon juice and rind. They are then baked and served with a spicy hot seasoning poured over the top. This dish is sumptuous served with vegetable side dishes such as potato in mustard oil.

Serves 4

4 rainbow trout, about 250g/9oz each, scaled and gutted

For the marinade:

4 tbsp mustard oil
1 tsp salt or to taste
1 tsp fennel seeds
½ tsp crushed dried chilli
grated rind and juice of 1 lemon
½ tsp ground turmeric

For the sauce:

2 tbsp mustard oil
½ tsp mustard seeds
1 medium onion, finely chopped
½ tsp crushed dried chilli
3 tbsp chopped fresh coriander (cilantro) leaves

PER PORTION Energy 368.8kcal/1542kJ; Protein 40.7g; Carbohydrate 9.1g, of which sugars 5.9g; Fat 19.2g, of which saturates 3g; Cholesterol 160mg; Calcium 114.5mg; Fibre 2g; Sodium 153mg.

1 Lay the fish on a flat surface and make three diagonal slits on each side. Put them in a shallow dish. Mix the marinade ingredients together and pour over the fish. Gently rub in the marinade, working it well into the slits. Set aside for 1 hour.

2 Preheat the oven to 180°C/350°F/Gas Mark 4. Line a roasting pan with foil and brush it generously with oil. Lay the fish in the pan and cook in the centre of the oven for 20 minutes.

3 For the sauce, heat the oil over a medium heat. When it is smoking, remove the pan from the heat and add the mustard seeds, then the onion. Fry the onion until translucent.

4 Add the crushed chilli and cook for 1 minute. Pour in 120ml/4fl oz/½ cup warm water and cook it for 2–3 minutes. Transfer the fish to a serving dish.

5 Add the fish juices to the onion sauce, then stir in the chopped coriander and cook for 1 minute. Spoon the sauce over the fish and serve with plain basmati rice.

Chicken with Stir-fried Onions and Shallots

Murgh do Piaza

This richly spiced chicken dish makes a delectable main course for a light summer dinner, and is delicious when accompanied by basmati rice and fresh vegetable side dishes. The onions are sautéed with the spices and tomatoes which adds a rich depth of flavour, and then the shallots are browned whole and added right at the end of the cooking time.

Serves 4

675g/1½lb skinned chicken thigh or breast fillets, cut into 5cm/2in cubes
juice of half a lemon
1 tsp salt or to taste
4 tbsp sunflower oil or olive oil
2 medium onions, finely chopped
1 tbsp ginger purée
1 tbsp garlic purée
1½ tsp ground coriander
1 tsp ground cumin
1 tsp ground turmeric
½–1 tsp chilli powder
225g/8oz canned chopped tomatoes, with their juice
1 tbsp ghee or 1 tsp unsalted (sweet) butter plus 2 tsp oil
8–10 small whole shallots
½–1 tsp garam masala
1 tbsp chopped fresh mint or 1 tsp dried mint
4–5 whole green chillies
2 tbsp chopped fresh coriander (cilantro) leaves

1 Put the chicken in a mixing bowl and add the lemon juice and salt. Mix thoroughly, cover the bowl and set aside in a cool place for around 30 minutes.

2 In a medium-sized pan, preferably non-stick, heat the oil and sauté the onions, ginger and garlic over a medium heat until the mixture begins to brown, about 7–8 minutes.

3 Add the coriander, cumin, turmeric and chilli powder and cook gently for about one minute, then add the tomatoes. Cook, stirring regularly, until the tomatoes reach a paste-like consistency and the oil separates from the paste.

4 Increase the heat to high and add the chicken. Cook, stirring constantly, for 4–5 minutes or until the chicken changes colour.

5 Pour in 250ml/8fl oz/1 cup warm water, bring it to the boil and reduce the heat to low. Cover and cook for 15–20 minutes, stirring the mixture occasionally for even flavour.

6 In a separate pan, heat the ghee or butter and oil over a medium heat. Add the shallots and stir-fry until they are lightly browned, then stir in the garam masala. Add this mixture to the chicken and stir over a medium heat until the sauce has thickened.

7 Add the mint, chillies and chopped coriander. Stir them in and cook for 1–2 minutes longer. Serve with naan bread and a vegetable side dish. A light cold beer makes a refreshing accompaniment.

PER PORTION Energy 401kcal/1678kJ; Protein 42.6g; Carbohydrate 18.2g, of which sugars 10.6g; Fat 18.3g, of which saturates 3.3g; Cholesterol 75mg; Calcium 99mg; Fibre 3.7g; Sodium 143mg.

Chicken in a Rich Buttercream Sauce

Murgh Makhani

Serves 4

For the chicken tikka:

675g/1½lb skinless chicken breast fillets, cut into 5cm/2in cubes
Juice of half a lemon
1 tsp salt or to taste
115g/4oz/½ cup Greek (US strained plain) yogurt
1 tbsp garlic purée
1 tbsp ginger purée
½ tsp ground turmeric
1 tsp garam masala
½ tsp chilli powder
2 tsp gram flour or cornflour (cornstarch)
1 tsp sugar
3 tbsp sunflower oil or olive oil
50g/2oz/4 tbsp butter, melted
5–6 metal or bamboo skewers

For the sauce:

150g/5oz/10 tbsp unsalted (sweet) butter
5cm/2in cinnamon stick, broken up
3 cardamom pods, bruised, and 4 cloves
2 green chillies, roughly chopped
1 tbsp garlic purée
1 tbsp ginger purée
400g/14oz canned chopped tomatoes
2 tbsp tomato purée (paste)
2 tsp sugar
2 tsp salt
1–2 tsp chilli powder
200ml/7fl oz/¾ cup warm water
2 tsp dried fenugreek leaves
150ml/5fl oz/½ cup double (heavy) cream

PER PORTION Energy 793kcal/3293kJ; Protein 45.8g; Carbohydrate 14.2g, of which sugars 9g; Fat 64.4g, of which saturates 37.1g; Cholesterol 227mg; Calcium 102mg; Fibre 1.2g; Sodium 1491mg.

One of the most popular dishes in India, Murgh Makhani, or Butter Chicken, is an ingenious invention from creative Indian chefs who were seeking a way to re-heat tandoori chicken without drying it out. You can use any leftover tandoori chicken, usually cooked on the bone, or you can make up freshly cooked chicken, as here.

1 Put the chicken in a mixing bowl. Rub in the lemon juice and salt. Set aside for 30 minutes. Whisk the yogurt and stir in the remaining tikka ingredients, except the melted butter. Mix thoroughly and add to the chicken, then stir until fully coated with marinade. Cover and leave in the fridge for 2–3 hours or overnight. Bring to room temperature before cooking.

2 Pre-heat the grill (broiler) to high and lightly brush the skewers with oil. If using bamboo skewers, soak them in water for 30 minutes first to prevent them burning.

3 Thread the chicken pieces on to skewers, reserving the remaining marinade, and place on the grill pan. Cook 7.5cm/3in below the heat source for 5 minutes. Meanwhile, mix the leftover marinade with melted butter. Remove the chicken from the grill and brush generously with this mixture. Continue to cook for 3–4 minutes, until slightly charred. Turn the skewers over and baste with the remaining spiced butter. Cook for 2–3 minutes longer or until charred on the other side. Remove them from the heat and wrap them in foil to keep hot.

4 To make the sauce, gently melt half the butter in a pan. Add whole spices, then the ginger and garlic purées. Cook for 2–3 minutes. Add the remaining ingredients except the cream. Cover and simmer for 20 minutes.

5 Remove from the heat and allow to cool slightly, then purée the ingredients until smooth. Use a hand blender or push the sauce through a sieve (strainer).

6 Return the pan to the heat, and add the remaining butter and the cream. Let the mixture come to a slow simmer, then add the cooked chicken tikkas. Simmer for 5–6 minutes, remove from the heat and serve with any Indian bread or boiled rice.

Royal Style Marinated Leg of Lamb

Nawabi Raan

Typical of regal cuisine from the days of the 13th-century Mongolian warrior Chengiz Khan, this recipe is a joy to make – once the meat is marinated, you are free to get on with other dishes. The yogurt used in the marinade must be thick – Greek yogurt is ideal, but if you cannot find this, use plain, thick-set full-fat yogurt, strained through a muslin cloth to remove the excess water.

Serves 4–6

3kg/6¾lb/10oz leg of lamb
120ml/4fl oz/½ cup red wine vinegar
1¼ tsp salt, or to taste

For the marinade:

50g/2oz/½ cup blanched almonds
pinch of saffron threads, pounded
1 large onion, roughly chopped
5cm/2in piece of fresh chopped root ginger
4–5 garlic cloves, roughly chopped
75g/3oz/⅓ cup Greek (US strained plain) yogurt or thick natural (plain) yogurt
1 tsp chilli powder
1 tsp ground cumin
25g/1oz/2 tbsp butter, melted

For the sauce:

1 tbsp unsalted (sweet) butter
½ tsp ground cardamom
¼ tsp each freshly grated nutmeg
½ tsp ground black pepper
1 tbsp gram flour
2 tbsp brandy
105ml/3½fl oz/7 tbsp double (heavy) cream

For the garnish:

1 tbsp toasted flaked (sliced) almonds
1 medium red onion, cut into rings
sprigs of fresh mint and wedges of lime

1 Remove excess fat from the meat. Using a sharp knife, make small, deep incisions on both sides, scattered all over the leg, to allow flavours to penetrate. Pour over the vinegar and sprinkle on salt, then rub into the meat, working it into the cuts. Set aside for 1 hour.

2 Place all the marinade ingredients, except the butter, in a food processor, blending until smooth. Pour the marinade over the meat and rub all over the surface, working it well in. Cover and chill for 6–8 hours or overnight. Bring the meat to room temperature for 2 hours.

3 Preheat the oven to 180°C/350°F/Gas Mark 4. Put the marinated leg of lamb in a deep roasting pan. Scrape off remaining marinade from the dish and spread it over the meat. Pour in enough water to cover up to three-quarters of the meat's depth. Cover the roasting pan with foil and cook in the centre of the oven for 1 hour. Turn the joint and cook for another hour.

4 Remove foil and baste the meat with pan juices; return to oven and cook for 6–7 minutes, then baste with the melted butter. Cook for a further 6–8 minutes and remove from oven. Transfer meat to a serving dish. Allow to stand for 20–30 minutes, strain the juices and reserve.

5 To make the sauce, melt the butter over low heat. Add the cardamom, nutmeg and black pepper. Stir once, then pour in the strained stock. Blend the gram flour with a little water to make a pouring consistency. Pour this into the stock and reduce the sauce to the desired thickness. Add the brandy and cream, cook for 3–4 minutes and remove from the heat.

6 Spoon some sauce over the meat and sprinkle toasted almonds over the top. Serve the remaining sauce separately. Garnish the meat with onion rings, lime wedges and sprigs of mint.

PER PORTION Energy 661kcal/2746kJ; Protein 56.5g; Carbohydrate 4.1g, of which sugars 1.1g; Fat 46.5g, of which saturates 22g; Cholesterol 242mg; Calcium 66mg; Fibre 0.9g; Sodium 185mg.

Lamb in Rich Chilli-Tomato Sauce

Rogan Josh

One of the most popular lamb dishes in the Kashmir region of India, this sumptuous dish makes wonderful festive fare. It has a rich, red colour, achieved by using Kashmiri chilli powder, which is hot but not too pungent. Vegetable dishes such as cauliflower or aubergine make fabulous accompaniments.

Serves 4

- 675g/1½lb boned leg of lamb, cut into 2.5cm/1in cubes
- 2 tbsp red wine vinegar
- 1 tsp salt, or to taste
- 50g/2oz/4 tbsp ghee or unsalted (sweet) butter
- 2 tbsp sunflower oil or olive oil
- 2.5cm/1in piece of cinnamon stick
- 2 brown cardamom pods, bruised
- 5 cloves
- 1 large onion, finely chopped
- 2 tsp ginger purée
- 2 tsp garlic purée
- 1½ tsp ground coriander
- 2 tsp ground cumin
- 1 tsp ground turmeric
- ½–1½ tsp Kashmiri chilli powder
- 400g/14oz can tomatoes with their juice
- ½ tsp ground cardamom
- ½ tsp ground nutmeg
- 2 tbsp chopped fresh coriander (cilantro)

Cook's Tip

To substitute Kashmiri chilli powder, add beetroot (beet) juice to standard chilli powder.

PER PORTION Energy 557kcal/2334kJ; Protein 54.2g; Carbohydrate 20.4g, of which sugars 18.7g; Fat 29.5g, of which saturates 13.5g; Cholesterol 190mg; Calcium 139mg; Fibre 4.6g; Sodium 277mg.

1 Put the meat in a non-metallic bowl and add the vinegar and salt. Rub them well into the meat and set aside for about an hour.

2 Reserve 1 tbsp ghee or butter, then heat the remainder with the oil in a large, heavy-based pan over a low heat. Add the cinnamon, cardamom and cloves, and let them sizzle for about a minute so that the flavour seeps in.

3 Add the onion, increase the heat slightly, and cook for 5–6 minutes until it has softened. Add the ginger and garlic purées, and continue to cook, stirring frequently, until the mixture is tinged with a light brown colour.

4 Add the ground spices – coriander, cumin, turmeric and chilli powder – and cook for about a minute, then add half of the tomatoes. Cook over a medium heat until the tomato juice has evaporated and then add the remaining tomatoes. Continue to cook until the mixture resembles a thick paste and the fat separates from the paste.

5 Add the meat, and increase the heat to high, then cook until it changes colour. Add 150ml/5fl oz/⅔ cup warm water and bring the mixture to the boil. Reduce the heat to low, cover and simmer for 45–50 minutes, stirring occasionally.

6 In a small pan, melt the reserved 1 tbsp ghee or butter over a low heat and gently fry the cardamom and nutmeg for 25–30 seconds. Pour the spiced butter over the meat and stir in half the chopped coriander. Remove the pan from the heat and garnish with the remaining coriander. Serve with plain boiled basmati rice or naan bread, and a vegetable side dish, such as Cauliflower and Green Peas in Mustard Oil.

Vegetable Korma

Subziyon ka Korma

Korma-style cooking was originally used only for meat and poultry dishes, but it proved so popular that vegetarian and fish recipes were created later. Hard to resist, this colourful vegetarian dish is a combination of vegetables coated in a luxurious almond sauce, exotically spiced with cardamom and coriander. It is important to blanch the vegetables for just a few minutes before adding them to the sauce, so that they do not overcook. By using this method, they retain all their delicate natural flavours and colours. This dish goes well with basmati rice.

Serves 4

- 375g/13oz cauliflower, divided into 1cm/½in florets
- 115g/4oz carrots, cut into batons
- 115g/4oz fine green beans, cut into 5cm/2in pieces
- 375g/13oz potatoes, boiled in their jackets and cooled
- 50g/2oz blanched almonds, soaked in 150ml/5fl oz/⅔ cup boiling water for 20 minutes
- 4 tbsp sunflower oil or olive oil
- 2 medium onions, finely chopped
- 2 green chillies, seeded and finely chopped
- 2 tsp ginger purée
- 1 tbsp ground coriander
- ¼ tsp ground turmeric
- ½ tsp chilli powder
- 1 tsp salt, or to taste
- ½ tsp sugar
- 120ml/4fl oz/½ cup double (heavy) cream

1 Blanch all the vegetables separately – the beans for 3 minutes, the cauliflower for 3 minutes and the carrots for 5 minutes – then plunge them immediately into cold water. Cut the cooked potatoes into 2.5cm/1in cubes.

2 Purée the blanched almonds in a blender or food processor with the water in which they were soaked, and set aside.

3 In a heavy pan, heat the oil over a medium heat and add the onions, green chillies and ginger purée. Fry them for 10–12 minutes until they turn a light brown colour and stir them regularly.

4 Add the coriander, turmeric and chilli powder. Reduce the heat to a low temperature and fry for 1 minute.

5 Add the vegetables, salt and sugar. Pour in 150ml/5fl oz/⅔ cup warm water, stir once and then bring to the boil. Reduce the heat to low, add the cream and cook for 2–3 minutes, then serve.

PER PORTION Energy 381kcal/1577kJ; Protein 5.1g; Carbohydrate 20.9g, of which sugars 9.9g; Fat 31.4g, of which saturates 19.3g; Cholesterol 78mg; Calcium 95mg; Fibre 3.9g; Sodium 108mg.

Indian Cheese with Fenugreek and Spinach

Methi Chaman

Serves 4

225g/8oz paneer
4 tbsp sunflower oil or olive oil
1 large onion, roughly chopped
25g/1oz fresh root ginger, roughly chopped
4 large garlic cloves, roughly chopped
1 tbsp dried fenugreek leaves
1–2 fresh red chillies, chopped, and seeded if preferred
1 tsp ground cumin
1 tsp ground coriander
½ tsp chilli powder
½ tsp ground turmeric
150g/5oz chopped canned tomatoes with their juice
1 tbsp tomato purée (paste)
275g/10oz/2½ cups fresh spinach, chopped
½ tsp salt, or to taste
3 tbsp double (heavy) cream
½ tsp garam masala

PER PORTION Energy 296kcal/1227kJ; Protein 13g; Carbohydrate 15.6g, of which sugars 9.8g; Fat 21.4g, of which saturates 6.4g; Cholesterol 22mg; Calcium 211mg; Fibre 3.3g; Sodium 333mg.

The predominant flavour in this tasty savoury dish is of the dried fenugreek leaves. The paneer, Indian cheese, used contains the same amount of protein as meat, making it ideal for a vegetarian diet. The cheese is cut into cubes and sautéed until browned, before it is simmered in the sauce.

1 Slice the paneer lengthways into five slices, then cut each slice into 1cm/½in cubes.

2 In a non-stick frying pan, heat 1 tbsp of the oil over a medium heat and sauté the cubes of paneer until they are browned. Remember to take care as paneer tends to splutter in hot fat. Drain the cheese cubes on absorbent kitchen paper and allow to cool slightly.

3 Purée the onion, ginger, garlic, fenugreek and chopped red chillies in a food processor or blender until they are well blended.

4 Heat the remaining oil in a medium-sized pan. Add the puréed ingredients and cook over a medium heat, stirring regularly for 5–6 minutes, or until the ingredients begin to stick slightly to the bottom of the pan.

5 Reduce the heat to low and add the cumin, coriander, chilli powder and turmeric. Simmer for 30 seconds, then add the tomatoes, and cook over a medium heat, stirring regularly, until the tomatoes are pulpy and the juice has thickened.

6 Add 2–3 tbsp water and continue to cook for a further 2 minutes. Carefully stir in the tomato purée and the sautéed paneer cubes.

7 Add the spinach and salt, and stir continuously until the leaves have wilted. Reduce the heat to low and cook for 3–4 minutes.

8 Add the cream and garam masala and cook for 2–3 minutes then remove from the heat. Serve with naan.

Mustard Greens with Fresh Root Ginger, Chilli and Garlic

Sarson ka Saag

This delicious Punjabi side dish uses mustard greens that are first blanched and puréed, then mixed with fried onion, fresh root ginger, garlic and green chillies, and served with chilled unsalted butter.

Serves 4

- 450g/1lb fresh mustard or spring greens, finely chopped
- 250g/9oz fresh spinach leaves, finely chopped
- 5cm/2in piece of fresh root ginger, finely chopped or grated
- 4–5 large garlic cloves, finely chopped
- 2–3 green chillies, seeded and chopped
- 1 tsp salt or to taste
- 1 tsp dark brown sugar
- 1 tbsp fine cornmeal or polenta

For the spiced butter:

- 2 tsp ghee or unsalted (sweet) butter
- 2.5cm/1in piece of fresh root ginger, cut into julienne strips
- 2 fresh red chillies, seeded and cut into julienne strips
- ½ tsp chilli powder
- 40g/1½oz butter, chilled and cut into small cubes

1 In a heavy pan, bring 300ml/½ pint/1¼ cups water to the boil and add the mustard greens, spinach, ginger, garlic and green chillies. Bring the pan back to the boil, reduce the heat to low, cover and cook for 25–30 minutes. Cool the mixutre slightly before puréeing the leaves along with all the cooking liquid.

2 Transfer the puréed greens back in to the pan and place over a medium heat. When they begin to bubble, add the salt, sugar and cornmeal or polenta. Stir and cook over a low heat for 15–20 minutes, or until the excess moisture evaporates.

3 In a small pan or a ladle, heat the ghee or butter over a medium heat and add the ginger and red chilli slivers. Cook for about a minute, then stir in the chilli powder and pour the spiced butter gently over the greens.

4 Transfer the greens to a serving dish and top with the cubes of chilled butter. The sharp flavours of the dish are accentuated when accompanied by Punjabi Cornmeal Bread.

Cook's Tip

Mustard greens are available in Indian stores, but you can use spring greens (collards) and add a dash of prepared English (hot) mustard for an authentic Punjabi flavour.

PER PORTION Energy 138.5kcal/573.2kJ; Protein 4.9g; Carbohydrate 9.5g, of which sugars 7.8g; Fat 9.1g, of which saturates 5.5g; Cholesterol 23mg; Calcium 173mg; Fibre 4.1g; Sodium 172.5mg.

Serves 4

500g/1¼lb/4½ cups self-raising (self-rising) flour
1 tsp baking powder
1 tsp salt
2 tsp sugar
50g/2oz/4 tbsp softened butter
250ml/8fl oz/1 cup warm milk
melted butter, to glaze

Variation

Before cooking the naan, brush a little beaten egg or plain yogurt on the surface and sprinkle on flavourings such as cumin seeds, nigella seeds, poppy seeds, chopped garlic, chopped green chillies or fresh coriander (cilantro).

Tandoori Leavened Bread

Naan

This basic recipe for naan can be varied by adding your own toppings such as seeds, herbs and chillies. The perfect accompaniment for Indian curries, they also make a filling snack.

1 Sift the flour into a large mixing bowl and add baking powder, salt and sugar. Mix well, then rub in the butter. Gradually add the milk and mix until a dough is formed. Transfer to a pastry board and knead for 5 minutes. Cover with a damp cloth and leave to rest for 30 minutes.

2 Preheat the grill (broiler) to high for 8–10 minutes, then line a grill (broiling) pan with a piece of foil and brush over it with a little dab of oil.

3 Divide the dough into eight equal-sized balls and flatten into cakes. Roll each cake into a circle 13cm/5in in diameter, then gently pull the lower end to form it into the traditional teardrop shape. Roll again, maintaining the teardrop shape, into a 23cm/9in naan.

4 Place a naan in the grill pan and cook it 13cm/5in below the heat source for about 1½ minutes until it puffs up. Keep an eye on it as it can burn easily when it puffs up. Turn it over and grill for 1 minute or until brown patches appear.

5 Place the cooked naan on a clean towel and brush the surface with a little melted butter. Wrap it in the towel to keep hot while you finish cooking the other naans. Serve with any meat, poultry or vegetable curry dish.

PER PORTION Energy 630kcal/2666kJ; Protein 18.7g; Carbohydrate 117g, of which sugars 2.95g; Fat 13g, of which saturates 2.2g; Cholesterol 127mg; Calcium 246mg; Fibre 4.6g; Sodium 712mg.

Punjabi Cornmeal Bread

Makki ki Roti

This tasty bread is the mainstay of cooking in the Punjab and is simple to make. It is made using fine cornmeal, available from Indian grocers and health food stores. Alternatively, you can substitute polenta, which is widely available from supermarkets.

Makes 8

175g/6oz/1½ cups cornmeal

90g/3½oz/¾ cup plain (all-purpose) flour

½tsp salt

butter, to serve

Cook's Tip

You can substitute cornmeal with polenta. It is advisable to avoid quick-cook varieties which lack the flavour of slow-cook versions.

1 Mix the cornmeal, flour and salt together. Gradually add approximately 250–300ml/8–10fl oz/1–1¼ cups warm water and blend together until it forms a moist but firm dough, then transfer to a pastry board. Knead the dough until it is soft and pliable.

2 Cover the dough with a damp cloth and let it rest for 30 minutes. Meanwhile, preheat a cast-iron griddle or frying pan over a medium heat.

3 Divide into eight equal-sized balls. Rotate each ball gently between your palms, then flatten into a round cake 13cm/5in in diameter, patting and stretching gently with your fingertips. You may find it easier to place the cakes between layers of clear film (plastic wrap) before shaping.

4 Lift a cake gently from the film and place on the heated griddle. Cook for 1 minute and turn over with a thin spatula. When the bread has set, cook both sides until brown patches appear.

5 Remove from the griddle and spread butter on one side (as much or as little as you like). Serve with Mustard Greens, which makes a classic Punjabi meal.

PER PORTION Energy 119kcal/500kJ; Protein 3.1g; Carbohydrate 24.7g, of which sugars 0.2g; Fat 0.9g, of which saturates 0g; Cholesterol 0mg; Calcium 17mg; Fibre 0.8g; Sodium 123mg.

Indian Iced Dessert

Kulfi

Although described as an Indian ice cream, the ever-popular Kulfi has a much denser texture. Various nuts and fruits and even chocolate can be added to the basic mixture. In this quick kulfi recipe, an almond-based ice is topped with passion fruit for a fruity flavour.

Serves 4

50g/2oz/½ cup blanched almonds
400g/14oz/1¾ cups can of evaporated milk
300ml/½ pint/1¼ cups double (heavy) cream
115g/4oz/½ cup caster (superfine) sugar
½ tsp ground cardamom

To serve:

1 tbsp toasted flaked (sliced) almonds, or the pulp and seeds of 2 passion fruits

1 Soak the almonds in 120ml/4fl oz/½ cup of boiling water for 20 minutes.

2 Put the evaporated milk, double cream and caster sugar into a pan and place over a low heat. Stir until the sugar has dissolved. Remove from the heat and set aside until cold. Keep an eye on the mixture, and stir from time to time to prevent a skin forming. Alternatively, cover the surface with moistened baking parchment.

3 Purée the almonds in a food processor or blender with the water in which they were soaked, and add to the milk mixture along with the ground cardamom. Stir to mix well, then pour into Kulfi moulds or small freezer-safe containers. Freezer for at least 5–6 hours.

4 If you are using small containers, it will be easy to remove the Kulfi from them; for larger containers, leave the Kulfi sitting at room temperature for about 15–20 minutes before removing, then cut the block into the desired portions. Serve with the flaked almonds or squeeze passion fruit over the top of the Kulfi.

PER PORTION Energy 260kcal/1082kJ; Protein 10.9g; Carbohydrate 18.3g, of which sugars 18.1g; Fat 16.2g, of which saturates 7.8g; Cholesterol 40mg; Calcium 344mg; Fibre 0.6g; Sodium 171mg.

north-east india

The regional fare of the north-east is dominated by meat and dairy foods, though freshwater fish also adds variety. From succulent duckling and tangy fish dishes to fragrant basmati rice and coconut balls, the cooking of north-east India offers a colourful cornucopia of sumptuous flavours and textures.

North-east India

Seven states make up the region of north-east India. This is a picturesque, hilly country, again bordering on the eastern edge of the Himalayan mountains where they tower over Nepal, Bhutan and China. These states are all landlocked – the only access to the sea is via Bangladesh or Myanmar (Burma) – and so the main focus of regional cuisine is on meat and dairy products rather than fish. However, tasty freshwater fish from the Brahmaputra River and its tributaries makes a welcome variation in the diet.

Perhaps the best known of the north-eastern states, because of its association with the tea crop, is Assam. Peoples of distinctly different cultures and trends of civilization took shelter here – the Dravidians, Indo-Mongols, Tibetans and Burmese are among those who contributed to the creation of this unique community. The soil is fertile and the climate mainly benign. There are over 700 tea plantations in the state and approximately 55 per cent of their output is exported to other states in India and to other countries, making a staggering 15.6 per cent of the world's production of tea. The food in Assam is simple and nutritious, with fish and rice forming the major part of the daily diet, but vegetables are also very important. This is probably the only state in India where healthy eating is a way of life – very little fat is used in cooking and the emphasis is on fresh vegetables, plenty of greens, and pulses tempered with garlic, mustard oil and chillies. Dishes such as banana flower curry and a tomato and lemon curry known as Tenga are among the delicacies that the people of Assam have made their own. Another distinctive Assamese dish is Khar, which is typically made with raw papaya, raw banana or a mixture of peas, beans and a vegetable such as marrow. Khar is believed to aid the digestion, as it includes kharoni, an ingredient made from burnt banana ash.

The smaller, more remote states that cluster around the foothills of the Himalayas include Arunachal Pradesh, which owing to its easternmost position in this region is popularly known as 'the land of the rising sun'. It is situated directly in the shadow of the high snow-clad peaks, and its thick evergreen forests and meandering rivers make beautiful vistas. The majority of the population here have Tibetan and Burmese ancestors, and have maintained the culinary traditions of these countries. Meat, often lamb, goat or yak, forms the basis of many dishes, and cooks in Arunachal Pradesh do not use many spices – only garlic, ginger, chillies and locally grown aromatic herbs.

The other five small states of north-east India, Meghalaya, Manipur, Tripura, Nagaland and Mizoram, have similar climates and landscapes, with rolling hills and mountain peaks where agriculture is somewhat restricted because of the uneven terrain. Here, farming consists mainly of rearing meat for local consumption, and tea is the main export crop. However, a wide range of spices, fruit and vegetables is grown and makes for a delightfully fresh cuisine that is also very nutritious. One of the favourite vegetables in the north-east is yam, which is made into fritters or mixed with spinach, tomatoes and spices for an interesting side dish. Rice is the main staple food and many small paddy fields can be found in the valleys, ideally suited to the warm, wet climate.

Batter-fried Spinach Leaves

Paleng Sakor Pat Bhoja

In this easy-to-make dish, large, very fresh spinach leaves are dipped in a spicy gram flour batter and crisp-fried to a delectable finish. Every mouthful exudes a complex blend of chilli, cumin, nigella and turmeric to titillate the tastebuds.

1 Wash the spinach leaves carefully without damaging them. Trim the stems but leave approximately 2.5cm/1in stem on each leaf. Dry the leaves thoroughly on absorbent kitchen paper.

2 Sift the gram flour into a large mixing bowl and add the rest of the ingredients except the oil. Mix the dry ingredients well, then gradually add 175ml/6fl oz/¾ cup water. Continue to stir the mixture until you have a thick batter.

3 Heat the oil in a wok or other suitable pan for deep-frying over a medium to high heat. To check that the oil is at the right temperature, drop a tiny piece of the batter into the hot oil. If it floats to the surface immediately without browning, then the temperature is just right. If you have a cooking thermometer, make sure that the oil is at least 180°C/350°F.

4 Hold each leaf by its stem and dip it in the batter, making sure it is fully coated. The stem should also be coated with the batter. Fry two or three leaves at a time, depending on the size of your pan. Cook them until they are golden brown and crisp; this will only take 1–1½ minutes per batch. Drain on absorbent kitchen paper and serve immediately.

Serves 4

12 large spinach leaves
75g/3oz/⅔ cup gram flour
25g/1oz/2 tbsp ground rice
½ tsp ground turmeric
½ tsp chilli powder
1 tsp cumin seeds
1 tsp nigella seeds
½ tsp salt or to taste
oil for deep-frying

PER PORTION Energy 247kcal/1027kJ; Protein 3.2g; Carbohydrate 20.6g, of which sugars 0.9g; Fat 17.5g, of which saturates 1.9g; Cholesterol 0mg; Calcium 106mg; Fibre 0.9g; Sodium 21mg.

Serves 8

1kg/2¼lb yam
1 tsp salt or to taste
1 tsp ground turmeric
1–1½ tsp chilli powder
½ tsp aniseed seeds
25g/1oz/¼ cup gram flour, sifted
15g/½oz/1 tbsp ground rice
oil for deep-frying
relish, to serve

Spiced Yam Slices

Kath Alur Pokora

Lightly coated in spiced gram flour batter and crisp-fried, these yam slices make a delicious appetizer to serve as a first course for lunch or dinner. Yams are readily available in good supermarkets and Asian stores, and are a good source of protein and potassium.

1 Peel the yam and cut into 5mm/¼in thick slices. Some yams have rather thin ends and are quite thick in the centre, so cut the bigger slices in half. Soak the slices in cold water for 30 minutes, then drain them. Do not dry them as they need to remain moist.

2 Put the salt, turmeric, chilli powder, aniseed seeds, gram flour and ground rice in a large mixing bowl and mix well. Add the sliced yam pieces and mix until they are fully coated with the spiced gram flour mixture.

3 Heat the oil for deep-frying in a wok or other pan suitable for deep-frying, over a medium to high heat. Fry the yam slices in batches in a single layer, without overcrowding the pan, for 3–4 minutes or until they are crisp and golden brown.

4 Drain the yam slices on absorbent kitchen paper. Serve with a relish of your choice, such as mango chutney, a spicy pickle or cooling cucumber and yogurt raita.

PER PORTION Energy 335kcal/1415kJ; Protein 3.5g; Carbohydrate 53.1g, of which sugars 1.3g; Fat 13.7g, of which saturates 1.6g; Cholesterol 0mg; Calcium 39mg; Fibre 2.4g; Sodium 4mg.

Fish in Tangy Tomato Sauce

Masor Tenga

Meals in Assam always end with Masor Tenga, a dish made with tomatoes and lime juice along with a flavoursome sprinkling of whole spices. Quick and easy to make, this dish makes a refreshing, healthy and delicious choice for a dinner. Any firm white-fleshed fish can be used and the selection of spices can be varied. Here, an earthy flavour is imparted by using mustard and nigella seeds. Although traditionally fresh tomatoes are used in this recipe, canned tomatoes have been used here because of the lovely rich colour they add to the dish.

Serves 4

675g/1½lb fillets of tilapia, monk fish or other firm white fish
1 tsp ground turmeric
1 tsp salt or to taste
3 tbsp mustard oil
½ tsp black mustard seeds
½ tsp nigella seeds
10–12 fenugreek seeds
2 green chillies, sliced lengthways, and seeded if you prefer
2 small potatoes, about 200g/7oz, finely chopped or grated
250ml/8fl oz/1 cup warm water
400g/14oz chopped canned tomatoes with their juice
1 tbsp lime juice
1 tbsp chopped fresh coriander (cilantro) leaves
plain boiled rice, to serve

1 Cut the fish into 5cm/2in pieces and lay them on a large plate. Sprinkle half of the turmeric and half the salt over them and rub both gently into the fish.

2 Heat the oil over a medium to high heat until it starts to smoke but not burn (the oil must be very hot), then fry the fish fillets in batches until the edges turn brown. Drain the fish pieces on absorbent kitchen paper.

3 Take the pan off the heat and add the mustard seeds, nigella seeds and fenugreek seeds, followed by the chillies. Return the pan to the heat and add the potatoes. Fry these together until the potatoes are golden brown.

4 Add the remaining turmeric and salt, and pour in 250ml/8fl oz/1 cup warm water. Bring the pan to the boil, then reduce the heat to low and cook for a further 5–6 minutes or until the potatoes are tender.

5 Add the tomatoes and cook for an additional 5–6 minutes. Next, add the fried fish and cook for 5 minutes. Stir in the lime juice and chopped coriander, give them a brief swirl and remove from the heat. Serve with a large spoonful of plain boiled rice.

PER PORTION Energy 345kcal/1445kJ; Protein 23g; Carbohydrate 28.3g, of which sugars 5.6g; Fat 16.3g, of which saturates 4.2g; Cholesterol 144mg; Calcium 105mg; Fibre 2g; Sodium 338mg.

Roast Duckling

Poora Haah

Serves 4

4 duckling portions, about 675g/1½lb, skinned
1 tsp salt, or to taste
2 tbsp red wine vinegar
3 tbsp sunflower oil or olive oil
1 large onion, finely chopped
2 tsp ginger purée
2 tsp garlic purée
½ tsp ground cumin
1 tsp ground coriander
½ tsp ground turmeric
½ tsp chilli powder
200g/7oz chopped canned tomatoes, with their juice
½ tsp garam masala
2 tbsp chopped fresh coriander (cilantro) leaves
plain boiled rice, to serve

PER PORTION Energy 361kcal/1510kJ; Protein 37.5g; Carbohydrate 13g, of which sugars 7.2g; Fat 21.3g, of which saturates 3.5g; Cholesterol 193mg; Calcium 67.5mg; Fibre 1.9g; Sodium 204mg.

Although this succulent recipe is labelled 'roast duckling', the bird is not roasted in the traditional way – rather, it is sautéed until it takes on a rich brown colour, then simmered in a spicy sauce until it is tender. The duck can also be grilled over a barbecue and simmered in the sauce. Contrary to the Western method of leaving the inside of the duckling pink, with Indian cooking, the bird is cooked until it is tender and no traces of blood can be seen.

1 Lay the duckling portions on a large plate and rub in half the salt and all of the vinegar. Set aside for 30 minutes.

2 In a large frying pan, preferably non-stick, heat the oil over a medium to high heat and brown the duckling portions until they are well-coloured and a crust has formed on the surface. Drain on absorbent kitchen paper. You could brown the duckling in the oven or under a hot grill, if you wish, but first brush the pieces with some oil.

3 In the remaining oil, fry the onion over a medium heat until it is soft. Add the ginger and garlic purées, and stir-fry until the mixture begins to brown.

4 Add the cumin, coriander, turmeric and chilli powder. Stir-fry for 1 minute and add the tomatoes. Stir-fry for another 4–5 minutes, or until the tomatoes are reduced to a paste-like consistency and the oil separates from the spice paste.

5 Add the browned duckling portions to the pan and pour in 250ml/9fl oz/1 cup warm water with the remaining salt. Bring the pan to the boil, then reduce the heat to low and cover the pan. Cook gently over a low heat for 40–45 minutes or until the sauce has thickened to a paste-like consistency.

6 Stir in the garam masala and half the chopped coriander. Serve the dish garnished with the remaining coriander and accompanied by plain boiled rice.

Fragrant Basmati Rice with Spiced Liver

Jadoh

Hailing from Meghalaya, Jadoh is a famous dish that uses pork or liver as its central ingredient. It is cooked rather like a pilau with only onion, ginger, garlic and chilli for flavour. In this recipe, a few extra spices have been added in order to enhance the taste. Although the Khasi tribal people traditionally use locally grown red rice, basmati rice – which is easier to find in shops – can be substituted, adding another fragrant note to this rich culinary blend.

Serves 4

250g/9oz/1¼ cups basmati rice
500g/1¼lb pig's liver
25g/1oz unsalted (sweet) butter
4 tbsp sunflower oil
1 large onion, finely sliced
8 large garlic cloves, lightly crushed
2.5cm/1in piece of fresh root ginger, minced (ground) or finely chopped
2 fresh red chillies, sliced at an angle
2.5cm/1in piece of cinnamon stick
2 bay leaves
1 tsp salt, or to taste
1 or 2 green chillies, seeded and cut into julienne strips, to garnish

1 Wash the basmati rice thoroughly in several changes of fresh, cold water and soak it for 20 minutes, then leave it to drain well in a colander.

2 Simmer the liver whole for 5 minutes in hot, salted water, skimming off any scum from the surface. Drain and rinse the meat thoroughly.

3 When it is cool enough to handle, cut up the piece of liver into 1cm/½in thick cubes and set these aside for a moment.

4 In a heavy-based frying pan, heat the butter and 1 tbsp of the sunflower oil over a medium heat, then sauté the liver cubes in batches for 2–3 minutes. Remove the liver from the pan and set aside. Discard any oil in the pan.

5 In a separate pan, heat the remaining sunflower oil over a medium heat and add the onion, garlic, ginger and red chillies. Stir-fry until the onion begins to brown.

6 Add the liver, rice, cinnamon stick, bay leaves and salt. Pour in 500ml/17fl oz/2 cups warm water and bring it to the boil. Let this mixture boil steadily for 2 minutes, reduce the heat to very low, cover the pan and cook for 7 minutes longer.

7 Remove from the heat and let the pan stand undisturbed for 10–12 minutes. Fork through the rice gently and serve garnished with the strips of green chilli.

PER PORTION Energy 609kcal/2539kJ; Protein 33g; Carbohydrate 62g, of which sugars 5.6g; Fat 21g, of which saturates 7.4g; Cholesterol 340mg; Calcium 52mg; Fibre 1.4g; Sodium 160mg.

Beef Stew with Green Chillies

Bawngsa Rep Leh Hmarchapui Bai

Serves 4

675g/1½lb stewing beef
1 tsp salt
2 tbsp red wine vinegar
1 large onion, roughly chopped
5cm/2in piece of fresh root ginger, roughly chopped
8 garlic cloves, roughly chopped
1–2 fresh red chillies, roughly chopped, seeded if preferred
1–2 green chillies, roughly chopped, seeded if preferred
3 tbsp sunflower oil or plain olive oil
¼ tsp chilli powder
4–5 green chillies, slit lengthways
plain boiled rice, to serve

This recipe is characteristic of Mizoram cuisine, in that the huge variety of spices used elsewhere in Indian food are absent. This is perhaps because of its geographical situation: Mizoram is a landlocked area where the people have learned to live on locally available ingredients. Traditionally, ginger, garlic, onion and fresh green chillies are the only ingredients that are used in this recipe, but here, a little chilli powder and fresh red chillies have been added to enhance the taste and embellish the appearance of the dish. The method of marinating the beef in vinegar is not traditional, but tenderizing the meat before cooking allows the flavours of the other ingredients to penetrate. This delicious stew is best served with boiled rice or new potatoes.

1 Remove any excess fat from the meat and cut into 2.5cm/1in cubes. Put the meat into a mixing bowl and add the salt and vinegar. Mix well and set aside for 30–40 minutes.

2 Put the onion, ginger, garlic and both types of fresh chopped chillies in a food processor and process them together, using the pulse action, until finely minced (ground).

3 Heat the oil over a medium heat and add the onion mixture. Stir-fry for 3–4 minutes, then add the beef and chilli powder. Stir-fry for another 4–5 minutes.

4 Pour in 300ml/10fl oz/1¼ cups warm water. Bring this to the boil, reduce the heat to low and simmer for 1½ hours or until the meat is tender when pierced with a fork.

5 Add the green chillies, stir the stew and remove the pan from the heat. Easy and quick to prepare, this hearty stew makes an excellent meal served simply with plain boiled rice, which absorbs the spicy and earthy flavours of the beef.

PER PORTION Energy 423kcal/1758kJ; Protein 41.7g; Carbohydrate 8.2g, of which sugars 5.8g; Fat 24.9g, of which saturates 7.7g; Cholesterol 102mg; Calcium 42mg; Fibre 1.4g; Sodium 117mg.

Cauliflower, Green Pea and Potato Curry

Phoolkobi, Motor Aru Alur Jool

The Hindu culinary rules dictate that no meat should be eaten on particular days of the religious calendar. This highly spiced vegetable curry is often prepared for religious festivals and other special occasions. It also makes a lovely light lunch.

1 Halve or quarter the potatoes according to their size – the pieces should be quite chunky so that they do not fall apart during cooking.

2 Divide the cauliflower into 2.5cm/1in florets, then blanch them briefly and plunge them in cold water to prevent further cooking.

3 Heat the oil in a large, non-stick pan over a medium to high heat and brown the potatoes in two to three batches until they are well browned and form a crust on the surface – they will look a bit like roast potatoes. Drain them thoroughly on absorbent kitchen paper.

4 In the same oil, fry the onion, ginger, garlic and chillies over a low to medium heat, stirring regularly, until the mixture begins to brown.

5 Add the ground turmeric and coriander, cook for 1 minute and then add the tomatoes, fried potatoes and salt. Pour in 400ml/14fl oz/1⅔ cups warm water. Bring this to the boil, reduce the heat to low, then cover and cook for 15 minutes.

6 Drain the cauliflower and add to the pan with the coated potato mixture. Add the peas, cook for 5 minutes, remove from the heat and serve garnished with coriander.

Serves 4

500g/1¼lb potatoes
1 small cauliflower or 350g/12oz cauliflower florets, with outer stalks removed
3 tbsp sunflower oil or olive oil
1 large onion, finely sliced
1 tsp ginger purée
1 tsp garlic purée
2 green chillies, chopped, seeded if preferred
½ tsp ground turmeric
1 tsp ground coriander
175g/6oz fresh tomatoes, chopped
1 tsp salt, or to taste
115g/4oz frozen garden peas
1 tbsp chopped fresh coriander (cilantro), to garnish

PER PORTION Energy 276kcal/1153kJ; Protein 9.7g; Carbohydrate 37g, of which sugars 11.6g; Fat 10.9g, of which saturates 1.5g; Cholesterol 0mg; Calcium 89mg; Fibre 6.5g; Sodium 33.8mg.

Serves 4

For the fritters:

115g/4oz/½ cup red split lentils

125g/4¼oz/½ cup skinless split mung beans

1 tsp fennel seeds

2 green chillies, roughly chopped, and seeded if you prefer

15g/½oz/¼ cup fresh coriander(cilantro) leaves and stalks

½ tsp salt or to taste

¼ tsp bicarbonate of soda (baking soda)

oil for deep-frying

For the sauce:

2 tbsp mustard oil

¼ tsp black mustard seeds

¼ tsp cumin seeds

¼ tsp fennel seeds

¼ tsp nigella seeds

6–8 fenugreek seeds

2 green chillies, sliced lengthways, and seeded if you prefer

2 small potatoes, finely chopped or grated

½ tsp ground turmeric

400g/14oz chopped canned tomatoes with their juice

½ tsp salt or to taste

1 tbsp lime juice

1 tbsp chopped fresh coriander leaves

plain boiled basmati rice, to serve

PER PORTION Energy 360kcal/1,510kJ; Protein 14g; Carbohydrate 51.3g, of which sugars 8.3g; Fat 12.3g, of which saturates 1.4g; Cholesterol 0mg; Calcium 119.2mg; Fibre 5.3g; Sodium 25.8mg.

Lentil Fritters in Spiced Tomato Sauce

Borar Anja

This recipe comes from Assam, the land of rich natural resources and world-renowned tea. The lentils are soaked and ground to a coarse paste with chillies and spices. Spoonfuls of the mixture are then fried in hot oil and simmered briefly in a tangy tomato sauce. You can make the fritters in advance and store them in the fridge.

1 Wash the lentils and soak them together with the mung beans for 3–4 hours. Drain and put them in a food processor. Add the remaining fritter ingredients except the oil. Add 3 tbsp water and blend the mixture until smooth.

2 Heat the oil in a wok over a medium heat. Add the lentil mixture, 1 tsp at a time and fry them until they are golden brown. Drain on absorbent kitchen paper.

3 To make the sauce, heat the oil over a medium heat until smoking. Remove the pan from the heat and add the mustard seeds, cumin seeds, fennel seeds, nigella seeds, fenugreek seeds and green chillies. Add the potatoes and return the pan to the heat. Stir-fry the potatoes until they are well browned. Stir in the turmeric, followed by the tomatoes and salt. Pour in 300ml/10 fl oz/1¼ cups warm water and bring to the boil. Reduce the heat to low and simmer for 3–4 minutes or until the potatoes are tender.

4 Add the fritters to the sauce and cook for 3–4 minutes. Add the lime juice and coriander leaves and remove from the heat. Serve with plain boiled basmati rice.

Fresh Tomato Chutney with Palm Sugar, Mustard and Chilli

Bilahir Oambal

With its distinctive sweet, hot and slightly tart taste, Bilahir Oambal is an enticing side dish that will enhance any Indian meal. A small spoonful during the meal makes the subsequent dishes even more enjoyable, presenting a different dimension to the tastebuds. A little goes a long way, but leftovers will keep in the refrigerator.

Serves 4

- 2 tbsp sunflower oil or olive oil
- ½ tsp black mustard seeds
- ½ tsp nigella seeds
- 500g/1¼lb tomatoes, skinned and chopped
- 1¼ tsp salt, or to taste
- 50g/2oz palm sugar (jaggery), grated (see Cook's Tip below)
- 2 tsp ground cumin
- 50g/2oz/⅓ cup seedless raisins

1 In a medium-sized pan, heat the sunflower or olive oil over a medium heat. When it is hot, but not smoking, add the mustard seeds.

2 As soon as the mustard seeds begin to pop, add the nigella seeds followed by the chopped tomatoes. Stir and reduce the heat slightly. Cover the pan and cook for 5 minutes.

3 Stir in the salt, jaggery and cumin, cover again and cook for an additional 5 minutes.

4 Add the raisins and cook, uncovered, for 9–10 minutes, over low to medium heat until the chutney has thickened. Stir regularly to distribute the ingredients evenly.

5 Remove from the heat, cool and serve cold with any Indian meal. Stored in a moisture-free, airtight jar in the refrigerator, this condiment should keep well for 3–4 weeks.

Cook's Tip

Palm sugar (jaggery) has a sweet, wine-like taste. To substitute palm sugar, use the same amount of light brown sugar.

PER PORTION Energy 154kcal/650kJ; Protein 1.2g; Carbohydrate 25.6g, of which sugars 25.6g; Fat 5.9g, of which saturates 0.8g; Cholesterol 0mg; Calcium 21.2mg; Fibre 1.5g; Sodium 560mg.

Serves 4

675g/1½lb yam
1 tsp ground turmeric
1 tsp salt, or to taste
4 tbsp mustard oil
1 tsp ginger purée
1 tsp garlic purée
2 green chillies, chopped, and seeded if you prefer
½ tsp ground cumin
250g/9oz spinach, finely chopped
150g/5oz fresh tomato, finely chopped

PER PORTION Energy 243kcal/1037kJ; Protein 5.2g; Carbohydrate 55.9g, of which sugars 3.4g; Fat 1.5g, of which saturates 0.3g; Cholesterol 0mg; Calcium 142mg; Fibre 4g; Sodium 587mg.

Golden Yam Cubes with Spinach

Kath Alu aru Paleng Sakor Torkari

Very popular in Assam and the rest of north-east India, this appetizing dish is easy to prepare and extremely nutritious. To make this dish, the yam is cut into small cubes and browned in perfumed, spicy mustard oil. The spinach is then quickly added in, and the yam cooks in the spinach juice. Finally, a sprinkling of turmeric is added to enhance the yam's beautiful golden colour.

1 Peel the yam and cut into 1cm/½in cubes. Soak in cold water for 30 minutes, drain and dry the cubes with a cloth. Sprinkle in half the turmeric and half the salt, and mix well.

2 Heat the oil over a medium heat and fry the yam cubes in two to three batches, until they are golden brown. Remove them with a slotted spoon and drain on absorbent kitchen paper.

3 In the oil that remains in the pan, fry the ginger, garlic and green chillies for 1–2 minutes. Stir in the cumin and add the remaining turmeric and the fried yam cubes, followed by the spinach leaves. Stir-fry together until the spinach has wilted, then add the tomatoes along with 200ml/7fl oz/¾ cup warm water.

4 Stir in the remaining salt and cook for 4–5 minutes, or until the water has been absorbed by the yam. This dish makes a great accompaniment for any meat, poultry or fish curry.

Plain Boiled Rice

Boga Bhaat

This absorption method of cooking plain rice, which is prevalent at so many Indian meals, offers an easy and healthy option. The important thing to remember when preparing rice is always to wash it in several changes of water until the water runs clear. This helps to remove milling starch and impurities which can sometimes create digestive disturbances. Whenever possible, soak the rice for 15–20 minutes before cooking, then drain. Last, but not least, once the lid goes on the pan, do not lift it until the cooking time is over. Of course, rice can also be cooked by draining excess water but this also removes many nutrients.

Serves 4

275g/10oz/1⅓ cups basmati rice

1 tsp butter

½ tsp salt

1 Wash the rice in several changes of water and then soak it for 20 minutes. Drain well.

2 In a medium-sized pan, bring 550ml/18fl oz/2½ cups water to the boil and add the butter, salt and the drained rice. Bring it to the boil and let it boil steadily for 1 minute.

3 Reduce the heat to low and cover the pan tightly. Cook for 8–9 minutes and switch off the heat source. Leave the pan to stand undisturbed for 10–12 minutes.

4 Fluff up the rice with a fork and serve with a main course or vegetable side dishes.

PER PORTION Energy 256kcal/1071kJ; Protein 5.1g; Carbohydrate 54.9g, of which sugars 0g; Fat 1.4g, of which saturates 0.7g; Cholesterol 3mg; Calcium 13mg; Fibre 0g; Sodium 255mg.

Makes 16

225g/8oz/1 cup desiccated (dry unsweetened shredded) coconut
250ml/8fl oz/1 cup full-fat (whole) milk
150g/5oz/¾ cup caster (superfine) sugar
1 tsp ground cardamom

Coconut Balls

Narikolor Laddu

Snow-white coconut balls, scented with ground cardamom, are made during all kinds of festivals in the Assam and Bengal regions of India. Narikolor Laddu are similar to coconut ice, but the process of making them is much simpler. For an irresistible treat, dip some of the balls into melted, rich dark chocolate and cool.

1 Put the coconut, milk and sugar in a non-stick pan and cook over a medium heat until the sugar has dissolved, stirring frequently to prevent the milk scalding.

2 Reduce the heat to low and cook, stirring constantly, for 35–40 minutes or until the coconut stops sticking to the bottom and sides of the pan. Stir in the teaspoon of ground cardamom and remove the mixture from the heat.

3 Make the balls while the coconut is still hot. Have a bowl of cold water ready and dip your hand in it, then pick up a lime-sized portion and place it in the palm of your hand. Shape the coconut mixture into a neat ball by pressing it down with your fingers. Repeat with the remaining mixture. Serve the balls as party treats or with coffee after dinner.

PER PORTION Energy 132kcal/551kJ; Protein 1.3g; Carbohydrate 11.5g, of which sugars 11.5g; Fat 9.3g, of which saturates 7.9g; Cholesterol 2mg; Calcium 26mg; Fibre 1.9g; Sodium 13mg.

east india

From sultry and sweet curries, to silky cheese curd desserts, the cooking tradition of east India provides an astounding variety of healthy, hearty and subtly delicious dishes. In more recent history, dishes have become enriched with locally grown spices including the five-spice mix panchforon, created by Bengali cooks.

East India

The eastern states of India are dominated by Bengal, with its capital city Kolkata (formerly Calcutta). Here the influence of Anglo-Indian food can still be found, many years after the end of British rule. The Bengali people are proud of their own rich cultural heritage – the poet Rabindranath Tagore is one of their most famous celebrities – and Bengali cuisine is part of this artistic tradition. Although the use of spices was fairly minimal here until medieval times, the Bengalis have developed a subtle cuisine using ingredients available in their own region. Locally grown spices such as fresh ginger, turmeric, mustard and sweet (bell) peppers are used to add flavour, and the characteristic five-spice mix known as panchforon was invented by Bengali cooks.

Plenty of fish and shellfish are caught in the Bay of Bengal, and this helped the Bengalis to create a stunning range of fish recipes which are renowned all over India. Dairy products such as yogurt, paneer and ghee are used imaginatively to create fabulous sweet and savoury recipes. But perhaps Bengal's greatest contribution to the food heritage of India is its magnificent spectrum of desserts, which are famous all over the nation. Sweets such as Gulab Jamoon (fried milk puffs in sugar syrup), Sandesh, a kind of soft fudge made of fresh cheese, and milky cardamom- and cinnamon-scented rice pudding are among the recipes that have made the reputation of Bengali cooks.

The wide fields of Bihar in the north of the region are dominated by the eastern sweep of the Himalayas, and by the magnificent Ganges River, which meanders slowly down from the mountains to emerge in Bangladesh (the independent Muslim state that was once part of Bengal). In landlocked Bihar, the climate is very hot in the summer and very cold in the winter, but wheat is grown and bread is as popular as rice. The daily diet in Bihar consists of rice, flat bread stuffed with spicy vegetables, lentils, raw vegetables and pickles. Thick and creamy yogurt is made by boiling the milk and then cooking it until it reduces to half its quantity, and as a result, the yogurt has a low water content and is smooth, delicious and very nutritious. The people of Bihar are very fond of ghee (clarified butter) and tend to use it freely in cooking instead of oil. They also maintain the thrifty tradition of preserving fresh food for future use, and this is usually done by drying summer vegetables in the fierce sun or preserving them as pickles.

The state of Orissa lies in the tropical zone and enjoys equable temperatures. Rice predominates in these lower, wetter areas of East India, where the climate is ideal for its cultivation. Sugar cane, coconuts and turmeric are the other main crops. However, the state is frequently hit by natural calamities such as cyclones, floods and droughts, which badly affect people's livelihoods as the population relies heavily on agriculture. The long coastline of Orissa at the northern edge of the Bay of Bengal means that fish and shellfish are a major part of the diet, and they are often cooked in fragrant coconut-based sauces. During the heat of the summer a delicious cool dish consisting of fermented rice and home-made yogurt is a great favourite in Orissa as it helps to lower the body temperature.

Meat-filled Potato Cakes

Alur Chop

Created by Indian chefs during the British Raj, this delicious snack consists of spicy minced meat packed into mashed potato casings, which are deep-fried in breadcrumbs for a lovely crunchy texture.

Makes 14 cakes

For the filling:

3 tbsp sunflower oil or olive oil
½ tsp black mustard seeds
½ tsp nigella seeds
1 large onion, finely chopped
2 tsp ginger purée
2 tsp garlic purée
2 green chillies, finely chopped and seeded
350g/12oz lean minced (ground) lamb/beef
1 tsp ground cumin
1½ tsp ground coriander
½ tsp ground turmeric
200g/7oz chopped canned tomatoes
75g/3oz/¾ cup frozen garden peas
½ tsp salt or to taste
½ tsp garam masala
2 tbsp chopped coriander (cilantro)

For the potato cakes:

1kg/2¼lb floury potatoes, skins left on
½ tsp salt, or to taste
1 large (US extra large) egg
2 tbsp milk
2 tbsp plain (all-purpose) flour
115g/4oz/2 cups golden breadcrumbs
oil for deep-frying

PER PORTION Energy 270kcal/1126kJ; Protein 9.3g; Carbohydrate 23g, of which sugars 3.4g; Fat 16.3g, of which saturates 2.7g; Cholesterol 29mg; Calcium 36mg; Fibre 1.8g; Sodium 99mg.

1 Heat the oil over a medium heat. When it is hot, but not smoking, add the mustard seeds followed by the nigella seeds. Add the onion and stir-fry until translucent. Add the ginger, garlic, green chillies and minced meat. Increase the heat slightly and stir-fry until the minced meat is dry and begins to brown slightly.

2 Add the ground spices and stir-fry gently for 1 minute, then add the tomatoes, peas and salt. Stir-fry over a medium heat until the tomato juice has evaporated, but the mixture is still quite moist. Stir in the garam masala and chopped coriander and remove from the heat. Allow to cool and divide into 14 equal portions.

3 Boil the potatoes with their skins on, then peel and mash them – floury potatoes are best for this recipe. Add the salt and mix in well, then divide the mashed potato into 14 equal portions.

4 Beat the egg and the milk together and then set them aside.

5 Take a portion of the mashed potato and flatten it into a neat cake, then make a depression in the centre to form a cup shape. Fill this cavity with a portion of the minced meat mixture, leaving about 5mm/¼in around the border. Next, press the entire circular border together to cover the minced meat, seal it completely and gently press it down to form a neat cake that is about 1cm/½in thick.

6 On a large, flat plate, dust the cakes in the flour, then dip them in the egg and milk mixture and roll carefully in the breadcrumbs.

7 Heat the oil in a wok or other pan suitable for deep-frying. Fry the cakes until they are crisp and golden brown, then drain them well on absorbent kitchen paper. Serve as a first course with a salad garnish or at buffet parties with a fruity chutney of your choice.

Spicy Chicken-and-Egg Rolls

Kathi Roll

These wickedly piquant chicken-filled tortilla rolls are the Indian version of 'fast food' – but so much more tasty! They make a delicious appetizer and also work extremely well as a light lunch.

Serves 4

675g/1½lb boneless chicken thighs or breast fillets, skin removed
3 tbsp sunflower oil or olive oil plus extra for brushing over
1 large onion, finely chopped
2 tsp ginger purée
2 tsp garlic purée
½ tsp ground turmeric
½–1 tsp chilli powder
1½ tsp ground coriander
¾ tsp salt or to taste
1 tbsp lemon juice
½ tsp garam masala
2 tbsp chopped fresh coriander (cilantro)
5 x 25cm/10in diameter tortilla wraps
5 medium (US larg) eggs

To serve:
1 medium red onion, finely sliced
1 tbsp chopped fresh coriander (cilantro)
1 green chilli, finely chopped (optional)
1 tbsp lemon juice

1 Cut the chicken pieces into cubes small enough to be cooked completely by the stir-fry method. Heat the oil over a medium heat and fry the onion for 3–4 minutes until translucent, then add the ginger and garlic. Stir-fry until the mixture is lightly browned.

2 Add the chicken and increase the heat to high. Stir-fry for 3–4 minutes and add the turmeric, chilli powder, ground coriander, salt and lemon juice. Stir-fry for a further 4–5 minutes, then stir in the garam masala and chopped coriander. Remove from heat but keep the mixture hot.

3 Place a heavy frying pan over a low heat and brush with oil. Beat an egg lightly. Place a tortilla wrap on the pan and spread the egg on top of this. Keep stirring and spreading the egg until it begins to set. Next, divide the chicken mixture into five equal portions and spread a portion on one half of the tortilla.

4 Mix the red onion, chopped coriander, chilli, if using, and lemon juice together and top the chicken with a little of this mixture. Roll up the tortilla and turn it over to allow the join to seal. Make the remaining rolls in the same way. Cut each roll in half diagonally and serve.

PER PORTION Energy 349kcal/1464kJ; Protein 34.7g; Carbohydrate 26.5g, of which sugars 4.9g; Fat 12.4g, of which saturates 2.3g; Cholesterol 60mg; Calcium 90mg; Fibre 2.1g; Sodium 191mg.

Fish in Aromatic Sauce with Vegetables

Macher Jhol

This well-loved dish from West Bengal is flavoured with mustard oil and a five-spice mix known as 'panchforon' – a combination of five whole spices that produces an unforgettable aromatic taste.

Serves 4–5

- 675g/1½lb fillets of tilapia or other firm white fish, cut into 5cm/2in pieces
- 1 tsp ground turmeric
- 1 tsp salt or to taste
- 4 tbsp mustard oil
- ¼ tsp black mustard seeds
- ¼ tsp cumin seeds
- ¼ tsp fennel seeds
- ¼ tsp nigella seeds
- 5–6 fenugreek seeds
- 2 bay leaves
- 2 dried red chillies, left whole
- 2 fresh green chillies, chopped
- ½ tsp ground cumin
- 1 tsp ground coriander
- 75g/3oz chopped canned tomatoes, with their juice
- 115g/4oz potatoes, cut into 1cm/½in cubes
- 115g/4oz aubergine (eggplant), cut into 1cm/½in pieces
- 50g/2oz/½ cup frozen garden peas
- 2 tbsp chopped fresh coriander (cilantro)
- plain boiled rice, to serve

1 Lay the fish on a large plate and gently rub in half the turmeric and half the salt. Set aside. Heat 2 tbsp of the mustard oil over a medium to high heat, and when it is almost smoking, switch off the heat source and immediately add the mustard seeds, followed by the cumin, fennel, nigella and fenugreek seeds. Add the bay leaves, and the red and green chillies.

2 Return the pan to the heat and add the cumin, coriander and remaining turmeric. Stir over a medium heat for 30 seconds and then add the tomatoes. Cook for 4–5 minutes.

3 Add in all the potato cubes and the aubergine pieces, along with about 350ml/12fl oz/1½ cups warm water and the remaining salt. Bring the pan to the boil, then reduce the heat to low, cover and cook for 15 minutes, stirring occasionally.

4 Meanwhile, heat the remaining oil in a frying pan, preferably non-stick, until almost smoking. Fry the fish in batches until well browned and drain on absorbent paper. Add the fried fish to the curry along with the peas. Cook for 4–5 minutes, then stir in the chopped coriander and remove from the heat. Serve with plain boiled rice.

PER PORTION Energy 242kcal/1011kJ; Protein 27.1g; Carbohydrate 7.4g, of which sugars 1.4g; Fat 11.9g, of which saturates 1.5g; Cholesterol 0mg; Calcium 184mg; Fibre 1.2g; Sodium 83mg.

Serves 4

275g/10oz/1⅓ cups basmati rice
4 tbsp sunflower oil or olive oil
5cm/2in piece of cinnamon stick, halved
6 green cardamom pods, bruised
4 cloves
2 bay leaves, crumpled
1 large onion, finely sliced
2 tsp ginger purée
1 green chilli, finely chopped, and seeded if preferred
½ tsp ground turmeric
1 tsp salt, or to taste
1 tbsp chopped fresh coriander (cilantro)
250g/9oz cooked and peeled prawns (shrimp)
sprigs of coriander leaves, to garnish

PER PORTION Energy 440kcal/1835kJ; Protein 17.9g; Carbohydrate 64.1g, of which sugars 5.6g; Fat 12.4g, of which saturates 1.3g; Cholesterol 122mg; Calcium 94mg; Fibre 1.4g; Sodium 123mg.

Prawn Pilau

Chingrir Pulao

Bengal is renowned for its fish and shellfish, and this pilau from Goa combines tasty prawns with a very simple preparation method. A flavoursome meal in itself, the dish also fits easily into a spread that includes meat, poultry and vegetable dishes as well.

1 Wash the rice in several changes of cold water and soak for 20 minutes. Leave to drain.

2 In a heavy-based pan, heat the oil over a low heat and add the cinnamon, cardamom, cloves and bay leaves. Stir-fry the ingredients gently for 25–30 seconds and then add the onion. Increase the heat to medium, and fry until the onion is beginning to brown, around 7–8 minutes, stirring regularly to prevent the spices from burning.

3 Add the ginger purée and chilli and continue to fry until the onion is well browned.

4 Add the turmeric, salt, chopped coriander, prawns and rice. Stir gently to mix the ingredients. Stir-fry for 2–3 minutes, then and pour in 475ml/16fl oz/2 cups hot water. Bring this to the boil and let it cook, uncovered, for 2–3 minutes. Reduce the heat to low, cover the pan tightly and cook for another 7–8 minutes.

5 Remove from the heat and let the dish stand for 5–6 minutes to absorb the flavour. Fluff up the pilau with a fork and transfer it to a serving dish. Garnish with sprigs of coriander.

Chicken Curry Anglo-Indian Style

Murgir Jhol

This recipe uses plenty of curry powder to give it a real bite. When made with pieces of chicken on the bone, it becomes a beautifully classic 'Anglo-Indian' curry, best served with a helping of plain boiled rice to moderate the spicy flavours.

Serves 4

- 675g/1½lb chicken leg or breast joint pieces on the bone
- ½ tsp ground turmeric
- 1 tbsp plain (all-purpose) flour
- 1 tsp salt, or to taste
- 1 large onion, roughly chopped
- 2.5cm/1in piece of fresh root ginger, roughly chopped
- 4–5 garlic cloves, roughly chopped
- 4 tbsp sunflower oil or olive oil
- 1½ tbsp curry powder
- ½ tsp chilli powder (optional)
- 175g/6oz fresh tomatoes, chopped
- 2 tbsp chopped fresh coriander (cilantro)
- plain boiled rice, to serve

1 Skin the chicken and separate the legs from the thighs. If you are using breast meat, cut each one into three pieces. Mix the turmeric, flour and salt together and rub this mixture into the chicken. Set aside to rest while you prepare the other flavourings.

2 Put the onion, ginger and garlic in a food processor to make a purée; alternatively, you can pound them together into a paste using a mortar and pestle.

3 Heat the sunflower oil in a medium-sized pan and add the puréed ingredients. Cook over a medium heat, stirring regularly, for 8–10 minutes.

4 Add the curry powder and chilli powder, if using, and cook for 2–3 minutes. Add around 2 tbsp water and continue to cook for a further 2–3 minutes.

5 Add the chicken, increase the heat to medium-high and stir until the chicken begins to brown. Add 425ml/15fl oz/1¾ cups warm water, bring it to the boil, cover and reduce the heat to low. Cook for another 35–40 minutes and add the tomatoes. Cook for 2–3 minutes longer, stir in the chopped coriander and remove from the heat. Serve with plain boiled rice.

PER PORTION Energy 392kcal/1632kJ; Protein 24.3g; Carbohydrate 12.5g, of which sugars 7.3g; Fat 27.6g, of which saturates 5.8g; Cholesterol 135mg; Calcium 67mg; Fibre 2.6g; Sodium 108mg.

Chicken Pilau

Murgir Pulao

Serves 4

275g/10oz/1⅓ cups basmati rice
2 tsp coriander seeds
1 tsp cumin seeds
1–3 dried red chillies, chopped
10 black peppercorns
2 tbsp white poppy seeds
1 tbsp sesame seeds
3 tbsp sunflower oil or olive oil
1 medium onion, finely sliced
2 tsp ginger purée
2 tsp garlic purée
½ tsp ground turmeric
450g/1lb skinned, halved chicken thigh fillets
75g/3oz/⅓ cup thick set natural (plain) yogurt, whisked
1 tsp salt, or to taste
1 tbsp ghee or unsalted (sweet) butter
2.5cm/1in piece of cinnamon stick
6 green cardamom pods, bruised
6 cloves
2 star anise
½ tsp salt, or to taste
1 tbsp toasted flaked (sliced) almonds, to garnish

PER PORTION Energy 487kcal/2035kJ; Protein 25.2g; Carbohydrate 65.5g, of which sugars 11.3g; Fat 13.7g, of which saturates 1.8g; Cholesterol 89mg; Calcium 55mg; Fibre 2g; Sodium 829mg.

Added to Bengal cuisine by the Mughals, this moist chicken dish has a long list of ingredients, but the final result is well worth the effort. Murgir Pulao tastes best when served hot and sprinkled with almonds.

1 Wash the rice in several changes of water and soak it for 20 minutes. Leave to drain.

2 Preheat a small heavy pan over a medium heat and add the coriander and cumin seeds. Reduce the heat to low, and dry roast the seeds for 25–30 seconds. Add the chillies, peppercorns, poppy and sesame seeds. Stir them for 25–30 seconds, then transfer them to a bowl. When cooled, grind the ingredients until fine, and set aside.

3 In a heavy-based pan, heat the oil over a medium heat and add the onion. Fry for about 5 minutes, until the onion is soft. Add the ginger and garlic and fry for a further 3–4 minutes. Add the turmeric and chicken, and increase the heat slightly. Cook until the chicken has changed colour. Add half the yogurt and cook for 2–3 minutes, stirring. Add the remaining yogurt and continue to cook for a further 2–3 minutes.

4 Add the ground ingredients and the salt, and reduce the heat to medium. Continue to cook for a further 2–3 minutes. Pour in 75ml/2½fl oz/⅓ cup warm water, reduce the heat to low and cook for another 5 minutes or until the liquid has evaporated, stirring all the while. Remove the pan from the heat and set aside while you prepare the remaining spices.

5 In a separate pan, heat the ghee or butter over a low heat and add the cinnamon stick, cardamom pods, cloves and star anise. Stir-fry until the cardamom pods have puffed up. Add the rice and salt, then stir, being careful to mix the spices well into the rice.

6 Pour in 475ml/16fl oz/2 cups warm water, bring it to the boil and let it boil steadily for about a minute. Reduce the heat to low, cover the pan tightly and cook for 7–8 minutes.

7 Switch off the heat source, remove the lid and pile the cooked chicken on top of the rice. Cover the pan again and let it stand, undisturbed, for 20 minutes. Gently mix the rice and the chicken with a metal spoon and serve immediately, garnished with toasted almonds.

Marinated Lamb Rib Chops

Rezala

Mutton, rather than lamb, is the traditional choice for this Muslim-influenced dish, which originated in the kitchens of one of the Mughal rulers near Kolkata (formerly Calcutta). However, this recipe uses lamb rib chops, as the cooking time is quicker. It makes a delectable meal when served with chunks of fresh naan or rice.

Serves 4

- 675g/1½lb lamb rib chops
- 1 tbsp red wine vinegar
- 1 tsp salt, or to taste
- pinch of saffron threads, pounded
- 1 tbsp hot milk
- 1 large onion, roughly chopped
- 5cm/2in piece of fresh root ginger, roughly chopped
- 4–5 cloves garlic cloves, roughly chopped
- 4 cloves
- ½ tsp black peppercorns
- 4 green cardamom pods
- 5cm/2in piece cinnamon stick, halved
- 4 tbsp sunflower oil or olive oil
- 1 large onion, finely sliced
- 175g/6oz/¾ cup natural (plain) yogurt, whisked
- 2 tsp gram flour
- 50g/2oz/4 tbsp butter, softened
- ½ tsp ground fennel
- ½ tsp dried ginger powder
- 3–4 fresh red chillies
- ½ tsp freshly grated nutmeg
- ½ tsp sugar
- 1 tbsp rose water

1 Put the lamb chops in a mixing bowl and rub in the vinegar and salt. Soak the saffron in the hot milk and set aside while you prepare the other ingredients.

2 Purée the onion, ginger and garlic in a blender or food processor. Put in a bowl and add a little water if necessary, then add the cloves, peppercorns, cardamom and cinnamon. Mix well and pour this marinade over the meat. Coat thoroughly, cover the bowl with clear film (plastic wrap) and leave to marinate for at least 3–4 hours or overnight in the refrigerator. Bring to room temperature before cooking.

3 Heat the oil over a medium to high heat and fry the sliced onions until they are browned. Remove them with a slotted spoon, squeezing out as much excess oil as possible, by pressing them to the side of the pan with the spoon.

4 In the remaining oil, fry the marinated lamb chops for 4–5 minutes, stirring frequently. Reduce the heat to low, cover and cook for 5–7 minutes.

5 Meanwhile, mix the yogurt, gram flour and butter together in a small pan and place over a low heat. Cook for 3–4 minutes, stirring constantly, then add the mixture to the lamb chops. Add the fennel and ginger powder and cover the pan. Cook until the chops are tender, about 45–50 minutes.

6 Add the chillies to the lamb chops along with the nutmeg and sugar. Cook for 1–2 minutes longer, then add the saffron milk and rose water (this can be bought from any large supermarket or Indian store). Stir well, remove from the heat and serve immediately with naan bread or a helping of plain boiled basmati rice.

PER PORTION Energy 610kcal/2529kJ; Protein 31.2g; Carbohydrate 7.4g, of which sugars 5g; Fat 51.1g, of which saturates 21.7g; Cholesterol 141mg; Calcium 124mg; Fibre 0.4g; Sodium 219mg.

Plantain Curry

Kaach Koler Kari

Serves 4

- 5 plantains
- 2 medium potatoes, about 225g/8oz
- 3 tbsp mustard oil
- ¼ tsp black mustard seeds
- ¼ tsp cumin seeds
- ¼ tsp nigella seeds
- ¼ tsp fennel seeds
- 6–8 fenugreek seeds
- 1 green chilli, chopped, seeded if you prefer
- 2.5cm/1in piece of fresh root ginger, minced (ground) or finely chopped
- ½ tsp ground cumin
- ½ tsp ground turmeric
- ¼–½ tsp chilli powder
- 75g/3oz fresh ripe tomato, skinned and chopped
- ¾ tsp salt or to taste
- ½ tsp garam masala
- sprigs of fresh coriander (cilantro), to garnish
- naan bread and/or plain boiled rice, to serve

PER PORTION Energy 340kcal/1437kJ; Protein 3.9g; Carbohydrate 63.3g, of which sugars 11.3g; Fat 9.8g, of which saturates 1.2g; Cholesterol 0mg; Calcium 32mg; Fibre 3g; Sodium 17mg.

In eastern India, plantains are very popular in curries or dusted with ground spices as a vegetable side dish. The earthy, squash-like flavour of the plaintain mixed with a variety of seeds, roots and spices, gives this curry a delightfully different flavour, perfect for a quick special dinner for family and friends. When shopping, plantains are occasionally referred to as 'raw' or 'green' bananas.

1 Peel the plantains with a small knife. Quarter them lengthways and cut them into 1cm/½in pieces. Soak them in cold water while you prepare the rest of the ingredients.

2 Cut the potatoes into pieces the same size as the plantains.

3 Heat 2 tbsp of the mustard oil over a medium heat until the smoke rises. Drain the plantains and dry them with a cloth. When the oil is ready, fry the plantain pieces in two batches until they begin to brown. Drain on absorbent kitchen paper.

4 Brown the potatoes in the same oil and drain on absorbent kitchen paper.

5 Add the remaining oil to the pan and heat until the smoke rises. Remove the pan from the heat and stir in the mustard, cumin, nigella, fennel and fenugreek seeds.

6 Next, stir in the chilli and ginger. Return the pan to the heat and stir-fry the ingredients for 25–30 seconds, then add the cumin, turmeric and chilli powder.

7 Stir well and add the tomato. Cook for 2–3 minutes and add the fried potatoes and salt. Pour in 400ml/14oz/1⅔ cups warm water and bring it to the boil. Reduce the heat to low, cover the pan and cook for 8–10 minutes or until the potatoes are tender.

8 Stir in the fried plantains and the garam masala. Cook for 2–3 minutes or until the plantains are tender, then remove from the heat and serve garnished with the sprigs of coriander. This dish is good with both naan bread and plain boiled basmati rice.

Vegetables in Ginger and Cumin Sauce

Labra

The original recipe for this dish was created using leftovers of different vegetables where there was too little to make up a single dish. It was so delicious that these days a combination of fresh vegetables are specially bought just to make Labra. Mustard oil is used here, but sunflower or olive oil may be used if you prefer.

Serves 4–5

- 4 tbsp mustard oil
- ¼ tsp black mustard seeds
- ¼ tsp cumin seeds
- ¼ tsp fennel seeds
- ¼ tsp nigella seeds
- 5–6 fenugreek seeds
- 2 bay leaves
- 1 medium onion, finely chopped
- 1 tsp ginger purée
- 2 green chillies, chopped, seeded if preferred
- ½ tsp ground turmeric
- ½ tsp chilli powder
- ½ tsp ground cumin
- 225g/8oz potatoes, cut into 2.5cm/1in cubes
- 1 small or ½ large butternut squash, cut into 2.5cm/1in cubes
- 1 large aubergine (eggplant), sliced lengthways and cut into 1cm/½in thick chunks
- 1 tsp salt, or to taste
- 75g/3oz/½ cup green beans, cut into 2.5cm/1in lengths
- 75g/3oz chopped canned tomatoes with their juice

1 Heat the oil in a large pan over a medium to high heat. When hot, remove from the heat source and add the mustard seeds, followed by the cumin, fennel, nigella, fenugreek seeds and bay leaves. Switch on the stove again, return the pan to the heat and add the onion, ginger and chillies. Stir-fry until the mixture begins to brown.

2 Stir in the turmeric, chilli powder and cumin. Cook for 30 seconds and add the potatoes, butternut squash, aubergine and salt. Pour in 450ml/16fl oz/2 cups warm water and bring it to the boil. Reduce the heat to low, cover and simmer for 20 minutes.

3 Meanwhile, blanch the green beans and plunge them into cold water. Add the beans to the pan with the tomatoes. Cook, uncovered, for 5–6 minutes over a medium heat until the sauce thickens and clings to the vegetables. This dish makes an ideal accompaniment to Chicken Curry Anglo-Indian Style.

PER PORTION Energy 190kcal/796kJ; Protein 7.2g; Carbohydrate 21.3g, of which sugars 5.5g; Fat 9.3g, of which saturates 1.4g; Cholesterol 0mg; Calcium 161mg; Fibre 3.4g; Sodium 45mg.

Stir-fried Spiced Lentils

Bhaja Muger Dhal

In this recipe, yellow split lentils are stir-fried with onions, chillies and cinnamon, before the cooking liquid is added. Golden turmeric provides an assertive yet subtle background taste to this dish.

Serves 4

- 225g/8oz/1 cup split yellow lentils
- 3–4 tbsp sunflower oil or olive oil
- 1 large onion, finely sliced
- 2.5cm/1in piece of cinnamon stick
- 4 green cardamom pods, bruised
- 1 bay leaf
- ½ tsp cumin seeds
- 1 tsp ground turmeric
- ½–1 tsp chilli powder
- 1 tsp salt or to taste
- 1 green chilli, seeded and cut into julienne strips, to garnish

1 Lentils often include tiny stones and other debris, so scan them carefully by spreading them in a large tray, then wash and drain them thoroughly.

2 Heat oil in a large, heavy, non-stick pan and add the onion. Fry, stirring regularly, for 8–10 minutes until well browned. Reduce the heat slightly during the last 3–4 minutes. Remove from the heat and lift out the onion with a slotted spoon, pressing down with another spoon to squeeze excess oil back into the pan. Drain the fried onion on absorbent kitchen paper.

3 In the remaining oil, sauté the cinnamon, cardamom, bay leaf and cumin seeds gently over a low heat for 30–40 seconds. Add the lentils and increase the heat to medium. Stir-fry for 4–5 minutes. Add the turmeric and chilli powder. Stir-fry for a further 2–3 minutes, add the salt and 120ml/4fl oz/½ cup lukewarm water. Increase the heat slightly and stir-fry until the water has evaporated. Add another 120ml/4fl oz/½ cup water and repeat the process once more, then add another 300ml/½ pint/1¼ cups warm water, and reduce the heat to low.

4 Reserve a little fried onion as garnish and stir the rest into the lentils. Cover the pan and cook for 12–15 minutes, until the lentils are tender – not mushy. Garnish with onion and chilli.

PER PORTION Energy 339kcal/1427kJ; Protein 23.7g; Carbohydrate 38.6g, of which sugars 4.9g; Fat 11g, of which saturates 7g; Cholesterol 35mg; Calcium 221mg; Fibre 3.7g; Sodium 788mg.

Griddle-cooked Flaky Bread

Dhakai Parota

A speciality from Dhaka, capital of Bangladesh, this flaky bread is highly addictive! The dough is rolled, spread with clarified butter, and then folded and re-rolled until several thin layers are formed. Here, the traditional clarified butter is used, but light olive or sunflower oil may be substituted if their flavours are preferred.

Makes 8

450g/1lb/4 cups plain (all-purpose) flour, plus extra for sprinkling
½ tsp salt
115g/4oz ghee or unsalted (sweet) butter
200ml/7fl oz/¾ cup warm water

1 Sift the flour into a large mixing bowl and rub in the salt and 1 tbsp of the ghee. Gradually add the water and mix until a dough is formed. Transfer this to a pastry board or work surface, and knead for 5–6 minutes until the dough is soft and pliable. Alternatively, you can make the dough in a food processor. Cover the bowl with a damp cloth and set the dough aside for 30 minutes to rest.

2 Divide the dough into eight equal-sized balls and make each one into a flat cake by turning it between the your palms and pressing it down. Roll each cake into a 13cm/5in diameter disc and spread about ½ tsp of ghee or butter on the surface.

3 Sprinkle a little flour on top of the ghee and, starting at the centre of the disc, make a slit to the edge of the disc. Roll from one end of the cut to the other, so that you end up with a cone shape. Press the cone down to make a cake again. Roll it out again, spread with ghee or butter as before, and repeat the entire process of sprinkling flour and making a cone. Once you have made the cone for the second time, press this down again and roll it out to a 13cm/5in diameter disc known as a parota.

4 Preheat a heavy cast iron or similar griddle over a medium heat and place a rolled disc on it. Allow the disc to cook for 2 minutes, then turn it over. Spread 1 tsp ghee or butter evenly on the surface and immediately turn it over again. Cook for an additional 2 minutes until the bread is browned all over underneath.

5 Spread 1 tsp ghee on the uncooked side. Turn it over and cook as above, until it is browned. Remove and place the bread on a wire rack. Cook the remaining parotas the same way. Serve with any meat or poultry dish.

PER PORTION Energy 293kcal/1232kJ; Protein 5.4g; Carbohydrate 43.7g, of which sugars 0.9g; Fat 12g, of which saturates 7.5g; Cholesterol 32mg; Calcium 81mg; Fibre 1.7g; Sodium 228mg.

Makes 16

275g/10oz/2½ cups plain (all-purpose) flour, plus a little extra for dusting
½ tsp nigella seeds
½ tsp salt
¼ tsp sugar
1 tbsp ghee, butter or margarine
175ml/6fl oz/¾ cup lukewarm water
sunflower oil for deep-frying

Deep-Fried Puffed Bread

Luchi

Delicious luchis are always made for Indian weddings and special occasions, served with meat curries or vegetable dishes. Allow three or four luchis per person, but make spares – they will be eaten!

1 Sift the flour into a large bowl and mix in the nigella seeds, salt and sugar. Rub in the ghee or butter. Gradually add water and mix until a stiff dough is formed, then transfer to a flat surface. Knead the dough for 4–5 minutes. Cover with a damp cloth and rest for 20 minutes.

2 Divide the dough into two equal parts and make eight equal-sized balls out of each. Press down between your palms to make flat cakes. Cover with a damp cloth again.

3 Heat the oil in a wok over a medium to high heat. While oil is heating, start rolling out the luchis by dusting each cake very lightly in flour. Roll out to 7.5cm/3in discs, taking care not to tear or pierce, as they will not puff up if damaged. Place them in a single layer on a piece of baking parchment and cover with another sheet of baking parchment.

4 When the oil has a faint shimmer of rising smoke, carefully drop in one luchi. As soon as it floats, gently tap around the edges of the luchi to encourage puffing. When it has puffed up, turn it over and fry the other side until browned. Drain on absorbent kitchen paper. Keep the fried luchis on a tray in a single layer. They are best eaten fresh, though they can be re-heated for 2–3 minutes in a hot oven. Serve with any meat, chicken or vegetable curry.

PER PORTION Energy 121kcal/506kJ; Protein 1.6g; Carbohydrate 13.4g, of which sugars 0.3g; Fat 7.2g, of which saturates 1.3g; Cholesterol 2mg; Calcium 24mg; Fibre 0.5g; Sodium 8mg.

Makes 16

150g/5oz/⅔ cup natural (plain) yogurt
400g/14oz can of evaporated milk
400g/14oz can sweetened condensed milk
½ tsp ground cardamom

PER PORTION Energy 470kcal/1980kJ; Protein 18.5g; Carbohydrate 68.7g, of which sugars 68.7g; Fat 15.3g, of which saturates 9.45g; Cholesterol 57mg; Calcium 625mg; Fibre 0g; Sodium 285mg.

Steamed Sweet Yogurt

Bhapa Doi

Hugely popular in Bengal, this yogurt makes a delicious dessert on its own or accompanied by other treats such as Silky Soft Cheese Fudge. It is also scrumptious served with seasonal fresh fruits such as Indian mango, summer fruits or ripe peaches. This recipe version is shorter than the traditional method, since it is abbreviated to cut the preparation and cooking time for busy cooks.

1 Preheat the oven to 120°C/250°F/Gas Mark ½. Put the yogurt in a large bowl and whisk it until smooth and glistening. Add the remaining ingredients and continue to whisk until all the ingredients are blended well.

2 Brush a 23cm/9in square baking dish with a little melted butter and pour the mixture into it. Fill a roasting pan or an ovenproof dish with hot water to the a depth of about 1cm/½in. Carefully set the baking dish into this, and bake the mixture in the centre of the oven for 30 minutes or until it is lightly set.

3 Remove from the oven and allow to cool. The dessert will become more firm as it cools, eventually reaching the correct consistency. Chill for 30–40 minutes before serving.

Silky Soft Cheese Fudge

Sandesh

With its snow-white appearance, subtle sweetness and refined taste, Sandesh is best enjoyed with a cup of tea or coffee. This basic recipe can be used to make variations of Sandesh, which come in different shapes and sizes, tastes and textures. Home-made cheese is essential for the recipe and can be made quite easily.

Makes 16

2.2 litres/4 pints/10 cups full-fat (whole) milk
juice of 1½ lemons
3 tbsp caster (superfine) sugar
¼ tsp ground cardamom
1 tbsp pistachio nuts, chopped

1 First make the cheese. Lightly brush a non-stick pan with oil (this will prevent the milk from sticking to the bottom) and pour in all the milk. Place over a medium heat and bring to the boil, watching it carefully to prevent it boiling over the top of the pan. When the milk begins to rise, add the lemon juice and reduce the heat to low.

2 Let the milk bubble until the whey has separated from the curdled milk. This will become obvious within a minute or so, as the milk becomes watery and the curds float on the top.

3 Strain the curdled milk through a piece of muslin (cheesecloth) and tie up the ends loosely, leaving the curds intact. Place the cloth in a sieve (strainer) over a bowl for 20 minutes, then place the curds on a pastry board or other flat surface.

4 Knead the curds for 8–10 minutes until the cheese is soft and smooth. At first, the cheese will be crumbly, but as you continue to knead it, using the knuckles and the heel of the hand, it will soon become smooth.

5 Place the cheese in a non-stick pan and add the sugar. Place the pan over a very low heat and stir for 8–10 minutes, or until the cheese stops sticking to the base and sides of the pan. Stir in the ground cardamom and remove the pan from the heat.

6 Grease a plate with a little melted butter and spread the cheese mixture on it. Shape it into a 15cm/6in square, about 1cm/½in thick.

7 Spread the chopped pistachio nuts on top and press them down gently. Let the mixture cool completely and then cut it into 5cm/2in squares. Serve the Sandesh on its own or with fresh fruits such as sliced mango, ripe peaches or pineapple.

PER PORTION Energy 107kcal/449kJ; Protein 4.6g; Carbohydrate 9.6g, of which sugars 9.6g; Fat 5.9g, of which saturates 3.4g; Cholesterol 19mg; Calcium 161mg; Fibre 0.1g; Sodium 81mg.

south india

The tart flavours of tamarind, lime and mango complement south India's rich stocks of meat, poultry and fresh seafood. Rice and coconut grow prolifically in the region's warm, humid conditions and add taste and texture to many delicious sweet and savoury recipes.

South India

The four states of Andhra Pradesh, Tamil Nadu, Karnataka and Kerala make up the region of South India. Foreign traders and explorers have often landed on these shores, attracted by the promise of a lucrative trade in exotic and costly items such as spices and silks. Traders from Europe and China later spread northwards throughout India, and were actively involved in setting up world trade routes. In the past, travelling between India and Europe was easiest and safest by sea, rather than trusting to the arduous and dangerous overland routes, and the welcoming southern Indian peninsula with its long coastline was an obvious starting point.

South India offers an inimitable range of food but with very clear regional variations – for example, the spicy broth known as Rasam will look and taste subtly different in Hyderabad, in the north of the region, from that made in Kerala on the south-west coast. Rice is the staple food, rather than the wheat bread of the cooler, drier north, and the southern climate with its warm temperatures and high humidity gives ideal conditions for rice production on a massive scale. Coconut is the other main crop of the south – every part of this serviceable plant is used, from the milk to the flesh, not forgetting the husk, which makes a good tough building material. The fine and delicate flavour of coconut permeates both sweet and savoury south Indian recipes.

In the large state of Karnataka, there are many flourishing coffee and tea plantations along the western coast. Farther inland, deep forests cover the slopes of the Western Ghats, the hills and mountains that run right down this side of the southern peninsula. Here ebony, cedar and sandalwood trees are grown, with their subtle perfumes and excellent potential for furniture making. The beautiful temple architecture of Karnataka, with its elaborate and organic forms, blends perfectly with this diverse landscape.

Andhra Pradesh, on the eastern seaboard, has quite a different climate, with the humidity of the monsoon making it ideally suited to rice production. The cuisine of Andhra Pradesh is unique among the southern states because of the influence of both Muslim and Mughal cooking, dating back to the invaders who battled over this land from the 14th century onwards. Chillies are one of the main crops of this region, and hot mixtures such as lime pickle are a favourite side dish.

Representing only 1.8 per cent of the total area of India, Kerala is the smallest state of South India. This strip of land along the Arabian Sea, leading right to the southern-most tip of India, has a beautiful coastline that stretches to 590 kilometres (367 miles). Fish and shellfish dishes cooked in spicy coconut milk, served with rice, are the staple diet of the region.

The history of the picturesque state of Tamil Nadu, on the south-eastern coast, is one of occupation by the Dravidian people, supposedly the descendants of the ancient Indus Valley civilization. Indications of people living and farming in this warm, wet land go back 6,000 years, and the Dravidian Tamil language is at least 2,000 years old. In later centuries Tamil Nadu became part of the European trade routes and a focus for the East India Trading Company. Many people in this state are vegetarians, partly for the purely practical reason that meat deteriorates quicker than vegetarian food in the muggy heat, and partly for religious reasons.

Stuffed Meat Patties

Shikampuri Kabab

These beautifully fragrant, melt-in-the mouth kebabs originated in Shikampur, near Hyderabad. The meat is flavoured with almond and coconut, and yellow split lentils are used as a binding agent.

Serves 4

500g/1¼lb lean minced (ground) lamb or beef
115g/4oz/½ cup yellow split lentils (channa dhal)
25g/1oz blanched almonds
25g/1oz desiccated (dry unsweetened shredded) coconut
2 tbsp sunflower oil or olive oil
1 medium onion, roughly chopped
5cm/2in piece of fresh root ginger, chopped
6 large garlic cloves, roughly chopped
2 dried red chillies, torn into pieces
2.5cm/1in piece of cinnamon stick, crushed
seeds of 6 green cardamom pods
4 cloves
8–10 black peppercorns
1 tsp cumin seeds
1 tsp salt
1½ tbsp lemon juice
15g/½oz coriander (cilantro) leaves and stalks
2 large eggs
1½ tbsp cornflour (cornstarch)
oil for shallow frying
mint leaves, to garnish

For the filling:

1 each small onion and tomato, chopped
1 green chilli, finely chopped
2 tbsp coriander (cilantro) leaves, chopped

1 Put the minced meat and the lentils in a pan and add 300ml/½ pint/1¼ cups water. Bring to the boil, reduce the heat to medium and cook, uncovered, for 10–12 minutes.

2 Add the almonds and coconut, reduce the heat slightly and continue to simmer until the lentils are tender but not mushy, about 10 minutes. Turn the heat up and cook for 5–6 minutes, until dry and crumbly. Remove from the heat and leave to cool.

3 Heat the oil in a small pan over a medium heat and fry the onion, ginger, garlic and red chillies for 6–7 minutes until browned. Finely grind the cinnamon, cardamom seeds, cloves, peppercorns and cumin in a coffee grinder.

4 Put the fried onion and ground spices in a food processor and add the cooked meat, salt, lemon juice, coriander and one egg. Add ground ingredients and process until well blended.

5 Divide the mixture into 16 equal portions. Have a bowl of cold water ready, moisten your palms and mould each portion of the kebab mix into a miniature cup shape.

6 Mix all the ingredients for the filling and divide into 16 equal portions. Fill the hollow in each kebab with a little of the filling mixture and cover it completely with the meat, then flatten it slightly to form a 2.5cm/1in thick cake.

7 Blend the cornflour with a little water and beat it with the second egg. Pour enough oil in a frying pan to measure about 1cm/½in in depth, and heat over a medium to high heat. Dip each kebab in the cornflour and egg mixture and fry until they are well browned, about 2–3 minutes on each side. Drain well on absorbent kitchen paper to reduce greasiness.

8 Garnish with fresh onion rings, sliced cucumber and tomato, lime wedges and sprigs of fresh mint and serve immediately, accompanied by naan or basmati rice.

PER PORTION Energy488kcal/2033kJ; Protein 27.9g; Carbohydrate 25.7g, of which sugars 3.7g; Fat 31.2g, of which saturates 7.4g; Cholesterol 238.5mg; Calcium 86.8mg; Fibre 3.1g; Sodium 140mg.

Tamarind-flavoured Lentil Broth

Rasam

Yellow split lentils or pigeon peas, known as toor dhal, are one of the most widely used ingredients in southern India. Spicy rasam originates in the hot region of Tamil Nadu, and is served in small cups to accompany a meal. The spices induce perspiration to cool down the body in summer, but the dish is equally good in the winter.

1 Wash the pigeon peas and place into a medium-sized pan. Add 1.5 litres/2½ pints/6¼ cups hot water, the salt, chillies and curry leaves. Place over a medium heat and gradually bring to the boil. Reduce the heat to low and simmer for 35–40 minutes.

2 Meanwhile, put the cumin seeds and the peppercorns together in a plastic bag and crush them lightly using the end of a rolling pin. Set aside.

3 Strain the soup well, pushing down the cooked lentils back into the broth. Mix well.

4 Heat the oil in a small pan until almost smoking. Remove the pan from the heat and add the mustard seeds, followed quickly by the asafoetida and chilli powder.

5 Stir in the crushed cumin seeds and peppercorns, then add the tomato and cook for 1 minute. Pour the seasoned oil into the soup, add the chopped coriander, tamarind or lemon juice and remove from the heat. Mix well and serve immediately.

Serves 4

75g/3oz/⅓ cup pigeon peas
1 tsp salt or to taste
2–3 whole fresh green chillies
6–8 curry leaves
1½ tsp cumin seeds
½tsp black peppercorns
2 tbsp sunflower oil or olive oil
½ tsp black mustard seeds
½ tsp asafoetida
¼–½ tsp chilli powder
1 small ripe tomato, finely chopped
1 tbsp coriander (cilantro) leaves, chopped
1½ tbsp tamarind or 2 tbsp lemon juice

PER PORTION Energy134kcal/560kJ; Protein 5.7g; Carbohydrate 13.7g, of which sugars 1g; Fat 6.8g, of which saturates 0.8g; Cholesterol 0mg; Calcium 24mg; Fibre 1.1g; Sodium 11mg.

Serves 4

675g/1½lb fillet of tilapia or any other firm white fish
2 tbsp lemon juice
1 tsp salt, or to taste
3 tbsp sunflower oil or olive oil
1 large onion, finely chopped
2 tsp ginger purée
1 tsp garlic purée
2 green chillies, finely chopped, and seeded if you prefer)
½ tsp chilli powder
½ tsp ground turmeric
400ml/14oz/1⅔ cups canned coconut milk
50g/2oz creamed coconut (⅔ cup coconut cream), cut into small pieces
toasted coconut flakes, to garnish
plain boiled basmati rice, to serve

PER PORTION Energy 366kcal/1528kJ; Protein 33.6g; Carbohydrate 13.7g, of which sugars 11.4g; Fat 20g, of which saturates 9.1g; Cholesterol 0mg; Calcium 269mg; Fibre 1.4g; Sodium 208mg.

Fish in Tamarind-laced Coconut Milk

Meen Molee

Both fish and coconut are found in abundance in and around the southern Indian coastline. Recipes such as this one are best made using white, firm-textured fish such as tilapia, monkfish or sole. However, it is just as successful when using large prawns. The coconut adds a fragrant richness to the dish.

1 Cut the fish into 5cm/2in pieces and lay them out on a large plate. Gently rub in half the lemon juice and half the salt. Set aside while preparing the other ingredients.

2 Heat the oil over medium heat, then add the onion and fry 5–6 minutes until the onion is soft, but not brown, about 5–6 minutes. Add the ginger, garlic and green chillies, and cook for a further 5–6 minutes until the mixture is a light golden colour.

3 Add the chilli powder and turmeric, cook for about 30 seconds, then pour in the coconut milk and add the creamed coconut. Add the remaining salt and lemon juice, and stir the mixture well until all of the creamed coconut has dissolved.

4 Carefully add the fish and simmer for 5–7 minutes or until the sauce has thickened. Remove from the heat and serve with plain boiled basmati rice.

Mixed Seafood in Spiced Coconut Broth

Cassoulet de Fruits De Mer

This popular and tasty dish hails from the once French-occupied region of Pondicherry; the recipe itself comes courtesy of Mehernosh Modi, one of the most talented Indian chefs in England. The assortment of seafoods in a piquant blend of chillies and spices makes the dish a multi-faceted feast for the tastebuds. It is delicious accompanied by basmati rice.

Serves 4

500g/1¼lb mixture of white fish fillets and assorted seafood, such as prawns (shrimp), mussels, scallops, crab claws, and squid
2 tbsp sunflower oil or plain olive oil
10–12 curry leaves
1 medium onion, finely chopped
200ml/7fl oz/¾ cup canned coconut milk
2 tsp lemon juice
salt to taste

For the purée:
4 dried red chillies
2.5cm/1in piece of fresh root ginger, chopped
3–4 garlic cloves, roughly chopped
2 tsp coriander seeds
1 tsp cumin seeds
½ tsp ground turmeric
6 black peppercorns
1 tbsp malt vinegar
sprigs of fresh coriander (cilantro), to garnish

1 Shell, trim and clean the seafood as required.

2 Grind the chillies, ginger, spices and other purée ingredients in a food processor or blender, or use a mortar and pestle. Heat the oil in a medium-sized shallow pan and add the curry leaves, followed by the chopped onion. Stir-fry over a medium heat until the onion is translucent, then add the puréed ingredients and sauté gently for 2 minutes.

3 Add the seafood, but not the white fish. Mix gently and cook for 2 minutes. Pour in the coconut milk, bring it to the boil, then add the white fish, lower the heat and simmer for 5–7 minutes until the white fish is cooked.

4 Add the lemon juice and salt and mix gently. Serve, garnished with sprigs of fresh coriander, accompanied by plain boiled basmati rice.

PER PORTION Energy 218kcal/913kJ; Protein 25.3g; Carbohydrate 13g, of which sugars 8.1g; Fat 7.7g, of which saturates 1g; Cholesterol 58mg; Calcium 64mg; Fibre 1.4g; Sodium 136mg.

Kerala Chicken Stew

Ishtoo

Here, chicken on the bone is cooked in a sumptuous, rich coconut broth. In Kerala, it is served with 'appam', a plain rice flour pancake, but it is also good accompanied by plain boiled basmati rice, which soaks up the tangy, green chilli-infused sauce.

Serves 4

675g/1½lb chicken leg or breast joints on the bone
4 tbsp sunflower oil or olive oil
2.5cm/1in piece of cinnamon stick
6 cardamom pods, bruised
4 cloves
12–15 curry leaves
1 large onion, finely chopped
2 tsp ginger purée
2 tsp garlic purée
2 green chillies, sliced at an angle
½ tsp ground turmeric
400g/14fl oz/1½ cups canned coconut milk
1 tsp salt, or to taste
500g/1¼lb medium potatoes,
175g/6oz/1½ cups frozen garden peas
plain boiled basmati rice, to serve

1 Skin the chicken joints, and cut each one into two pieces, then set aside.

2 Heat the oil in a large pan over a low heat and add the cinnamon, cardamom pods, cloves and curry leaves. Sauté these for 25–30 seconds and add the onion. Increase the heat to medium and fry until the onion is soft, about 5–6 minutes, then add the ginger, garlic and chillies and cook for 2–3 minutes longer to allow the flavours to blend.

3 Add the turmeric, stir well, then add the chicken. Increase the heat from medium to high and stir until the chicken browns. Pour in the coconut milk and add the salt, stir and mix well. Reduce the heat to low, cover and simmer for 15–20 minutes.

4 Halve the potatoes and pour in 250ml/8fl oz/1 cup warm water. Bring to the boil, reduce the heat to low, then cover and cook for an additional 20 minutes, or until the chicken is cooked and the potatoes are tender.

5 Add the peas, cook for 5 minutes longer and remove from the heat.

PER PORTION Energy 552kcal/2309kJ; Protein 40g; Carbohydrate 43.6g, of which sugars 16g; Fat 25.5g, of which saturates 6.9g; Cholesterol 192.5mg; Calcium 104.5mg; Fibre 5.4g; Sodium 271mg.

Chicken Cooked in a Coconut, Sesame Seed and Cashew Nut Sauce

Hyderabadi Murgh Korma

Unlike its north Indian counterpart, this chicken korma recipe calls for creamy coconut milk and chilli, and subtle flavour notes are added with a sprinkling of nutmeg and mace. Ghee is traditionally used here, but unsalted butter or oil can be substituted.

Serves 4

50g/2oz/½cup raw cashew nuts
200g/7oz/¾ cup thick set natural (plain) yogurt
2 tsp gram flour
2 tsp ginger purée
2 tsp garlic purée
½ tsp ground turmeric
½–1 tsp chilli powder
1 tsp salt, or to taste
675g/1½lb skinned chicken breast fillets, cut into 5cm/2in cubes
75g/3oz/6 tbsp ghee or unsalted (sweet) butter
2.5cm/1in piece of cinnamon stick
6 green cardamom pods, bruised
6 cloves
2 bay leaves
1 large onion, finely chopped
1 tbsp sesame seeds, finely ground
200ml/7fl oz/¾ cup canned coconut milk
¼ tsp freshly grated nutmeg
¼ tsp ground mace
Indian bread or boiled basmati rice, to serve

PER PORTION Energy 398kcal/1671kJ; Protein 46.4g; Carbohydrate 19.1g, of which sugars 12.5g; Fat 16g, of which saturates 3.8g; Cholesterol 76mg; Calcium 195mg; Fibre 2.1g; Sodium 265mg.

1 Soak the cashew nuts in 150ml/5fl oz/⅔ cup boiling water for 20 minutes.

2 Whisk the yogurt and gram flour together until smooth (do this thoroughly, otherwise the yogurt will curdle). Add the ginger, garlic, turmeric, chilli powder and salt. Mix well and pour the marinade over the chicken. Stir until the chicken is fully coated. Set aside for 30–35 minutes.

3 Reserve 1 tsp of ghee or butter and melt the remainder in a medium-sized pan over a low heat. Add the cinnamon, cardamom, cloves and bay leaves. Let these sizzle in the pan until the cardamom pods have puffed up.

4 Add the onion and increase the heat slightly. Sauté in the pan until the onion is translucent, then stir in the ground sesame seeds.

5 Add the marinated chicken, increase the heat to medium-high and stir until the chicken changes colour. Pour in the coconut milk and 150ml/5fl oz/⅔ cup warm water. Bring this to the boil, reduce the heat to low, cover and simmer for 20 minutes or until chicken is tender.

6 Meanwhile, purée the cashews with the water in which they were soaked and add to the chicken. Add ground sesame seeds. Simmer, uncovered, for 5–6 minutes until the sauce thickens.

7 Melt the 1 tsp of reserved ghee or butter in a small pan or in a steel ladle over a low heat. Add the grated nutmeg and ground mace, then cook gently for about 30 seconds. Pour the spiced butter over the chicken and stir to mix well. Serve with plain boiled basmati rice or any Indian bread. Cumin and Saffron-scented Wholemeal Flat Bread goes particularly well.

Minced Lamb Pilau

Tahari

This quick and easy pilau is traditionally made with minced mutton or lamb, but beef can also be used without changing the complex combination of spices. Like a fine wine, this richly spiced dish can be savoured on the tongue.

Serves 4

For the minced (ground) meat:
500g/1¼lb lean minced (ground) lamb
50g/2oz/¼ cup natural (plain) yogurt
3 tbsp sunflower oil or olive oil
1 large onion, finely sliced
2 tsp ginger purée
2 tsp garlic purée
2 green chillies, finely chopped
1 tsp ground cumin
1½ tsp ground coriander
½ tsp ground turmeric
½ tsp garam masala
½ tsp salt or to taste
75ml/3fl oz/5 tbsp single (light) cream

For the rice:
250g/9oz/1¼ cups basmati rice, washed and soaked for 20 minutes
pinch of saffron threads, pounded
2 tbsp hot milk
25g/1oz/2 tbsp ghee or unsalted (sweeet) butter
2.5cm/1in piece of cinnamon stick
5 cardamom pods, bruised
4 cloves
2 star anise
2 bay leaves
1 tsp salt, or to taste
2 hard-boiled eggs, quartered, to garnish

1 In a non-stick pan, cook the minced lamb over medium to high heat until the juices evaporate and the lamb is beginning to brown. Add the yogurt and cook over a low heat for 2–3 minutes, remove from the heat and set aside.

2 Heat the oil over a medium heat and add the onion. Stir-fry until the onion is well browned. Add the ginger, garlic and chillies, and stir-fry for 2 minutes, then add the cumin, coriander and turmeric. Stir-fry this for an additional 30 seconds before adding the browned meat and 150ml/5fl oz/⅔ cup of warm water.

3 Cook for 2–3 minutes, then add the salt, garam masala and cream. Cook for a further 2–3 minutes, then remove from the heat and keep warm.

4 Leave the rice in a colander to drain and soak the saffron strands in the hot milk.

5 Melt the ghee or butter over a low heat and add the cinnamon, cardamom, cloves, star anise and bay leaves. Stir-fry these until the cardamom pods have puffed up.

6 Add the drained rice and salt, stir to mix and pour in 550ml/18fl oz/2½ cups hot water. Let this boil steadily for 2 minutes, until the surface water has almost evaporated. Reduce the heat to low and sprinkle the saffron milk randomly over the surface.

7 Spread the spiced minced meat on top, making sure you cover all the grains of rice. Cover and cook for 6–7 minutes, keeping the heat as low as possible. Switch off the heat source, remove the pan from the heat and let the pilau stand for 15 minutes.

8 Gently stir with a metal spoon to mix the spiced minced meat and rice, transfer to a serving dish and garnish with the quartered hard-boiled eggs.

PER PORTION Energy Energy 609kcal/2544kJ; Protein 24.4g; Carbohydrate 79.6g, of which sugars 18.2g; Fat 21.5g, of which saturates 5.5g; Cholesterol 57mg; Calcium 70.2mg; Fibre 3.4g; Sodium 156mg.

Madras Meat Curry

Attu Erachi Kari

Madras (now Chennai) Christian and Muslim communities have an excellent range of meat and poultry dishes such as this tangy meat curry. Goat or mutton is the natural choice of ingredient, but lamb on the bone is also ideal for this provocatively flavoured dish.

Serves 4

- 675g/1½lb boned leg of lamb, fat trimmed and cut into 2.5cm/1in cubes
- 2 tbsp red wine vinegar
- 1 tsp ground turmeric
- 2 tsp garlic purée
- 2 tsp ginger purée
- 2 tsp chilli powder
- 1 tbsp tomato purée (paste)
- 1 tsp salt, or to taste
- 1 tsp black peppercorns
- 1 tsp coriander seeds
- 1 tsp cumin seeds
- ½ tsp black mustard seeds
- ¼ tsp fenugreek seeds
- 20 curry leaves
- 25g/1oz/⅓ cup desiccated (dry unsweetened shredded) coconut
- 4 tbsp sunflower oil or light olive oil
- 2.5cm/1in piece of cinnamon stick, halved
- 2 black cardamom pods
- 4 cloves
- 1 large onion, finely chopped

1 Put the meat in a non-metallic bowl and add vinegar, turmeric, garlic, ginger, chilli powder, tomato purée and salt. Mix thoroughly, cover the bowl and marinate for 4–5 hours.

2 Put the marinated meat into a heavy pan and add 150ml/5fl oz/⅔ cup water, bring it to a slow simmer, cover and cook until the water evaporates. Stir the pan several times during cooking so that the meat does not stick to the bottom of the pan.

3 Preheat a small heavy pan over a medium heat. Reduce heat to low, add the peppercorns, coriander, cumin, mustard and fenugreek seeds, and the curry leaves. Stir until the spices release their aroma, then add the coconut. Stir-fry until the coconut is lightly browned. Remove the spices from the pan and cool, then grind them until they are a very fine texture.

4 Heat the oil over a medium heat and add the cinnamon, cardamom and cloves. Leave to sizzle for 30 seconds, add the onion and brown. Add the ground ingredients and stir for 1 minute, then add the cooked meat. Add 150ml/5fl oz/⅔ cup warm water, cover and simmer for 10 minutes. Take off the heat and adjust the consistency with a little water.

PER PORTION Energy 524kcal/2180kJ; Protein 37.6g; Carbohydrate 13.8g, of which sugars 7.4g; Fat 36g, of which saturates 13.8g; Cholesterol 133mg; Calcium 65mg; Fibre 2.6g; Sodium 160mg.

Makes 18 cakes

275g/10oz/1½ cups semolina
1 tsp baking powder
½ tsp bicarbonate of soda (baking soda)
½ tsp crushed dried chillies
½ tsp salt, or to taste
400ml/14fl oz/1⅔ cups soda water
275g/10oz/1¼ cups thick-set natural (plain) yogurt

PER PORTION Energy 62kcal/264kJ; Protein 2.4g; Carbohydrate 13g, of which sugars 1.1g; Fat 0.4g, of which saturates 0.1g; Cholesterol 0mg; Calcium 32mg; Fibre 0.3g; Sodium 15mg.

Steamed Rice Cakes

Idli

These lovely rice cakes are popular all over the southern states of India. Two types of idlis are made, usually served with sambhar. One type uses a fermented rice and lentil mixture, and is rather time-consuming to prepare. Here, the cakes are made using semolina and then steamed in special steel idli moulds – however, an egg poacher and a steamer work equally well for this recipe.

1 Place the semolina, baking powder, bicarbonate of soda, chillies and salt in a mixing bowl and mix together well with a wooden spoon.

2 Gradually add the soda water and mix thoroughly. Beat the yogurt until smooth and add to the semolina mixture. Whisk until you have a smooth, thick paste, which should be the consistency of a cake mix, but slightly more moist.

3 Lightly brush the egg poachers with oil and then place 1½ tbsp of the idli mix into each poacher. Steam the rice cakes for about 10 minutes.

4 Ease the rice cakes away from the egg poachers and keep them warm while you steam the remaining cakes in the same way. These rice cakes make a delicious accompaniment to a Lentil, Tomato and Aubergine Curry.

Serves 4

225g/8oz/1 cup pigeon peas
½ tsp ground turmeric
1 large aubergine (eggplant)
1½ tsp salt, or to taste
1 tbsp coriander seeds
1 tsp cumin seeds
1–4 dried red chillies, broken up
½ tsp black peppercorns
½ tsp black mustard seeds
225g/8oz fresh tomatoes, chopped
2 tbsp tamarind juice or the juice of 1 lime
2 tbsp coriander (cilantro) leaves and stalks, finely chopped

Lentil, Tomato and Aubergine Curry

Sambhar

A partner dish for Steamed Rice Cakes, this Sambhar curry goes equally well with boiled basmati rice, and interestingly, with crusty white bread, too. The choice of vegetables is flexible – here aubergine and tomatoes are used. Pigeon peas are available from most Indian shops.

1 Put the lentils in a pan and add the turmeric and 1.2 litres/2 pints/5 cups water. Bring it to the boil, then reduce the heat to medium and cook for 3–4 minutes or until all the foam subsides. Reduce the heat to low, cover the pan and cook for 20 minutes.

2 Add the aubergine and salt, re-cover and continue to cook for a further 8–10 minutes or until the aubergine is tender when prodded with a fork.

3 Meanwhile, preheat a small heavy pan over a medium heat. Reduce the heat to low and add the coriander seeds, cumin seeds, chillies, peppercorns and mustard seeds. Stir and roast them for 30–60 seconds until they begin to release their aroma.

4 Remove them from the pan and leave to cool, then grind finely in a coffee or spice grinder. Add the spice mix to the lentils, followed by the tomatoes and tamarind or lime juice. Simmer for 2–3 minutes. Add the chopped coriander, remove from the heat and serve.

PER PORTION Energy 215kcal/914kJ; Protein 15.5g; Carbohydrate 36.2g, of which sugars 3.1g; Fat 2.1g, of which saturates 0.3g; Cholesterol 0mg; Calcium 69.8mg; Fibre 4.8g; Sodium 28mg.

Tamarind-laced Vegetables in Coconut, Coriander and Chilli Sauce

Avial

The wonderful flavours in this vegetarian main course make it very popular in southern India. Any combination of vegetables – peas, beans, cauliflower and other green vegetables – works very well.

Serves 4

125g/4½oz green beans, cut into 2.5cm/1in lengths
200g/7oz carrots, cut into 1cm/½in thick circles
225g/8oz potatoes, cut into 2.5cm/1in cubes
1 small aubergine (eggplant), about 200g/7oz, quartered lengthways and cut into 2.5cm/1in pieces
200g/7oz cauliflower, divided into 1cm/½in florets
½ tsp ground turmeric
1 tsp salt or to taste
2 tsp cumin seeds
50g/2oz/⅔ cup desiccated (dry unsweetened shredded) coconut
2–3 green chillies, chopped
200ml/7fl oz/¾ cup buttermilk
2 tbsp tamarind juice
2 tbsp sunflower oil or olive oil
½ tsp black mustard seeds
½ tsp cumin seeds
2–3 whole dried red chillies
6–8 curry leaves
¼ tsp asafoetida
1 tbsp fresh coriander (cilantro), chopped
plain boiled basmati rice, to serve

1 Put the green beans, carrots, potatoes and aubergine into a large pan and add 350ml/12fl oz/1½ cups hot water. Add the turmeric and salt. Bring to the boil, reduce the heat to low and cover the pan. Cook for 5–6 minutes, then add the cauliflower. Cover and cook until the vegetables are tender, but still firm (except the aubergine, which will be soft).

2 Meanwhile, heat a small heavy pan over a medium heat. Dry-roast the cumin seeds for 30–40 seconds. Remove from the heat and dry-roast the coconut and green chillies until the coconut is lightly browned. Transfer this to a plate and cool slightly. Put the roasted ingredients in a coffee grinder or blender and grind until fine-textured.

3 When the vegetables are ready, add the ground roasted ingredients, buttermilk and tamarind juice. Cook gently for 4–5 minutes, then remove from the heat. Heat the oil in a small pan over a medium heat. When hot, but not smoking, add the mustard seeds, followed by the cumin seeds, red chillies, curry leaves and asafoetida. Blacken the chillies, then pour the entire contents of the pan over the vegetables. Stir in the chopped coriander and remove the pan from the heat. Let the curry stand, covered, for 5–6 minutes. Serve with basmati rice.

PER PORTION Energy 252kcal/1050kJ; Protein 7.55g; Carbohydrate 22.5g, of which sugars 10.7g; Fat 15.5g, of which saturates 7.7g; Cholesterol 1.75mg; Calcium 119mg; Fibre 6.1g; Sodium 57mg.

Makes about 900g/2lb/4 cups

10–12 limes
1 tbsp salt
120ml/4fl oz/½ cup malt vinegar
250ml/8fl oz/1 cup vegetable oil
1 tsp asafoetida
10–12 garlic cloves, crushed
2.5cm/1in piece of fresh root ginger, grated or minced (ground)
10–12 curry leaves
2 tbsp black mustard seeds, finely ground
1 tbsp cumin seeds, finely ground
2 tsp fenugreek seeds, finely ground
2 tsp ground turmeric
2 tsp chilli powder
10 green chillies, halved
4 tsp salt
4 tsp sugar

Lime Pickle

Nimbu Achar

In India, pickles are served with the main course, unlike in the West, where they are served with poppadums at the start of a meal. Sharp lime pickle is one of the best-known Indian relishes. For this recipe, you will need ripe limes, with a slight yellow tinge on the skin. Avoid the dark green, unripe fruits as they are too acidic.

1 Wash the limes and dry them thoroughly with a cloth. Trim them, then cut them into quarters. Sprinkle the quarters with the salt and put them in a colander, placed over a bowl. Set aside for 2 hours, then transfer them to another bowl and add the vinegar. Stir until any remaining salt is dissolved and drain in the colander again.

2 Heat the oil in a pan over a medium heat and add the asafoetida, followed by the garlic, ginger and curry leaves. Allow them to brown in the pan slightly.

3 Add the ground seeds, turmeric and chilli powder, and stir-fry for 1 minute, then add the green chillies, salt and sugar. Stir-fry for 1 minute longer before adding the limes. Remove the pan from the heat and allow to cool completely.

4 Store the lime pickle in sterilized, airtight jars. To enjoy it at its best, leave the pickle in the jar for 4–5 weeks to mature before eating. The pickle will keep for 10–12 months.

Cook's Tips

- To sterilize jars for bottling, boil them in water for a minimum of 10 minutes.
- You'll need to plan ahead to make this pickle as it needs at least 4 weeks for the flavours to develop fully.

PER PORTION Energy 120kcal/492kJ; Protein 0.1g; Carbohydrate 0.3g, of which sugars 0.2g; Fat 13.1g, of which saturates 1.6g; Cholesterol 0mg; Calcium 9mg; Fibre 0.1g; Sodium 436mg.

Lemon-laced Rice

Naranga Choru

Lemon-laced rice is very popular all over India – its mild flavour is a perfect backdrop for any spicy curry. The dish also looks beautiful, with a pale yellow background for black mustard seeds, curry leaves and roasted cashew nuts. If you don't eat nuts, try adding a handful of toasted sunflower or pumpkin seeds instead.

Serves 4

225g/8oz/1¼ cups basmati rice
2 tbsp sunflower oil or olive oil
½ tsp black mustard seeds
10–12 curry leaves, preferably fresh
25g/1oz cashew nuts, broken
½ tsp ground turmeric
1 tsp salt, or to taste
2 tbsp lemon juice

1 Wash and rinse the rice two or three times in cold water, or until the water runs clear. Soak it for 15–20 minutes, rinse and drain it in a colander.

2 Heat the oil in a non-stick pan over a medium heat. When it is hot, but not smoking, add the mustard seeds, curry leaves and cashew nuts. Let them sizzle for 15–20 seconds.

3 Add the rice, turmeric and salt to the pan. Stir-fry the rice for 2–3 minutes, then add 475ml/16fl oz/2 cups hot water and the lemon juice. Stir the pan once, bring to the boil and continue to boil for about 2 minutes. Cover the pan tightly, reduce the heat and simmer gently for an additional 7–8 minutes.

4 Remove the pan from the heat and leave to stand, undisturbed, for 6–7 minutes. Fork through the rice, and serve immediately as an accompaniment to curry.

PER PORTION Energy 345kcal/1440kJ; Protein 6.9g; Carbohydrate 57.4g, of which sugars 0.4g; Fat 9.5g, of which saturates 1.4g; Cholesterol 0mg; Calcium 22mg; Fibre 0.2g; Sodium 20mg.

Apricot Dessert

Khubani ka Meetha

This mouthwatering dessert is simplicity itself. Fresh apricots are cooked in sugar until they are soft, cooled and then served with a dollop of whipped cream. A spicy note is added by cooking the apricots with star anise and cloves. Dried, ready-to-eat apricots can also be used, so that the dessert can be enjoyed all year round.

Serves 4

- 500g/1¼lb dried ready-to-eat apricots
- 4 cloves
- 2 star anise
- 115g/4oz/½ cup caster (superfine) sugar
- lightly whipped double (heavy) cream, to serve
- 2–3 tbsp toasted pistachio nuts, lightly crushed, to garnish

1 Put the whole apricots into a pan with 750ml/1¼ pints/3 cups water, cloves and star anise, and bring to the boil. Reduce the heat to low, cover the pan and simmer for 15 minutes, or until the apricots are soft. Stir at least twice during this time to ensure even cooking.

2 Remove the spices and discard them. Remove half of the apricots with a slotted spoon and set aside. Purée the remainder, along with the cooking juices, and return the purée to the pan.

3 Add the whole apricots and the sugar. Cook gently for around 3–4 minutes, then remove from the heat and allow to cool for about 30 minutes.

4 Put the required portions of the dessert in individual serving dishes and top with some freshly whipped cream. Sprinkle with the crushed pistachio nuts and serve.

PER PORTION Energy 306kcal/1305kJ; Protein 5.2g; Carbohydrate 74.4g, of which sugars 74.4g; Fat 0.8g, of which saturates 0g; Cholesterol 0mg; Calcium 106mg; Fibre 7.9g; Sodium 19mg.

Saffron-scented Rice Pudding

Pal Payasam

Even if rice pudding does not usually appeal to you, do not dismiss this one! It is quite different from the rice pudding made in the Western world. The richness of saffron, the fragrance imparted by the cardamom and nutmeg, and the crunchiness of the toasted nuts, make this pudding pure ambrosia. Serve it on its own, or team it with a fresh fruit, such as chopped mango, to complete the delicate flavours to perfection.

Serves 4

- 1.2 litres/2 pints/5 cups full-fat (whole) milk
- a good pinch of saffron strands, pounded
- 25g/1oz/2 tbsp ghee or unsalted (sweet) butter
- 6 green cardamom pods, bruised
- 2.5cm/1in piece of cinnamon stick
- 2 bay leaves
- 75g/3oz/⅓ cup basmati rice, washed
- 2–3 tbsp granulated (white) sugar
- 25g/1oz broken cashew nut pieces (optional)
- 3 tbsp double (heavy) cream
- 1 tbsp rose water
- a few fresh rose petals, washed, to garnish

Variation

Serve topped with chopped mango and crushed pistachio nuts, or any fresh fruit.

1 Soak the pounded saffron in the milk and set aside while preparing the other ingredients.

2 Melt the ghee or butter gently over a low heat and add the cardamom, cinnamon and bay leaves. Let them sizzle for 25–30 seconds.

3 Add the rice, the saffron-flavoured milk and saffron. Bring this to the boil, reduce the heat to low, and add the sugar and cashew nuts. Let the mixture bubble gently for 45–50 minutes, stirring frequently. Remove from the heat, then add the cream and rose water.

4 Serve in pretty ice cream dishes or bowls and garnish with the rose petals.

PER PORTION Energy 445kcal/1852kJ; Protein 12.5g; Carbohydrate 42.6g, of which sugars 26.8g; Fat 26g, of which saturates 14.6g; Cholesterol 71mg; Calcium 363mg; Fibre 0.2g; Sodium 235mg.

central india

From creamy kormas and crunchy spiced potatoes to delectable snacks and treats delicately flavoured with spices, nuts and seeds, the cuisine of central India holds many delicious surprises, with special dishes fit for a feast.

Central India

Central India is basically made up of one large state, Madhya Pradesh. This state is completely landlocked, with the Arabian Sea bordering the state of Gujarat to the west, and the Bay of Bengal bordering the state of Orissa to the east. The countryside is made up of beautiful rolling hills rising to 600m (2,000ft), where primeval forests still flourish. Central India is rich in natural resources; it contains the country's largest diamond mine, and because several major rivers flow through the state, it can provide a good part of its own electricity needs. Madhya Pradesh sits at the northern edge of the Deccan plateau, a huge area of volcanic basalt that stretches across the whole central and southern part of India. This rock was laid down in thick layers and the subsequent nutrient-rich volcanic soil has enabled the state to establish a hugely successful agricultural economy.

Madhya Pradesh has been a witness to the major external and internal influences that have been instrumental in shaping the country's culture and cuisine over the centuries. The state is a typical example of the diverse nature of Indian culture: beautiful Hindu and Sikh temples and Muslim mosques grace the region, with all the different religions and races now coexisting in relative harmony after the major upheavals of the 20th century.

The economy of central India relies mainly on agriculture. This fertile state is blessed by regular weather patterns – a hot summer from April to June, followed by the relief of torrential monsoon rains in July and August – which enables the farmers to plan which crops to grow and when to plant and harvest them. The main food crops of Madhya Pradesh are rice, wheat, sorghum and coarse millet, usually grown for the local markets. The typical flat bread of the region, made of sorghum, has become popular all over India. Oilseeds, cotton, sugar cane and soya beans are the main commercial crops, all of which are exported all over the world as well as being eaten locally. Although rice is a popular ingredient in central Indian cooking, wheat is the preferred staple in the drier western areas.

The main cities of Madhya Pradesh are Bhopal, Indore and Gwalior. Bhopal, the state capital, is situated in a beautiful area surrounded by lakes and hills. In the days of British domination, the state was ruled by various Indian princes, all of whom maintained strong loyalty to the British. Even now, in the 21st century, all three major cities still have Indian princes and princesses living in their palaces, and the traditions of an exotic royal cuisine are maintained among the wealthy.

The cuisine of Madhya Pradesh owes much to the nearby states of Gujarat, Rajasthan and Bihar, with their emphasis on the kind of dishes that best suit hot, dry areas. The luxurious dishes suitable for royal banquets, with edible gold and silver decorations, are not part of most people's everyday diet, of course. However, the daily food of central India does include plenty of variety in terms of the different spices, nuts and seeds that are added to the basic meat, fish and vegetables. The people of Madhya Pradesh also love to eat snacks, often dainty little morsels of vegetables deep-fried to perfect tenderness in a spicy batter, or tasty sweet cakes flavoured with cashew nuts.

Parsnip Patties

Shalgam Tikki

Central India is famous for its varied snacks, which Indians adore. Originally made from turnip (hence their Indian name), these delectable little patties use parsnips instead. The sweetness of this root vegetable works extremely well with the pungency of chillies and ginger.

Makes 14

2 tbsp sunflower oil or olive oil
675g/1½lb parsnips, peeled and chopped
1 large onion, roughly chopped
2.5cm/1in piece of fresh root ginger, roughly chopped
2–3 green chillies, chopped, and seeded if you prefer
1 large slice of white bread, (one or two days old)
1 large (US extra large) egg
½ tsp garam masala
¾ tsp salt, or to taste
15g/½oz fresh coriander (cilantro) leaves and stalks, roughly chopped
oil for shallow-frying

1 Heat the oil in a frying pan, preferably non-stick, and add the parsnips. Stir-fry over a medium heat until the edges of the parsnips have been tinged with a medium-to-dark brown colour, being careful not to burn them.

2 Add the onion, ginger and chillies. Stir-fry for 3–4 minutes and then remove from the heat.

3 Soak the bread in cold water and squeeze out all the water. Put the bread and the egg in a food processor or blender and blend until smooth. Add the parsnips, garam masala, salt and fresh coriander to the processor. Using the pulse action, blend all of the ingredients until smooth. Transfer to a bowl and chill the mixture for 35–40 minutes. Divide into 14 equal portions and flatten into 5mm/¼in thick cakes.

4 Cover the base of a frying pan to about 1cm/½in depth with oil and place on a medium heat. Fry the parsnip patties in batches until they are well browned on both sides. Drain on absorbent kitchen paper and serve immediately with mango chutney.

PER PORTION Energy 125kcal/521kJ; Protein 2g; Carbohydrate 9.9g, of which sugars 4.7g; Fat 8.9g, of which saturates 1.1g; Cholesterol 14mg; Calcium 35mg; Fibre 3g; Sodium 22mg.

Fish Baked with Cardamom, Cinnamon and Cloves

Dum Machchi

This fish recipe is cooked by sealing food into a heavy pan with a tight-fitting lid so that steam and flavour cannot escape. It is delicious accompanied by Basmati Rice with Caramelized Sugar.

Serves 4

675g/1½lb tilapia or monkfish fillets, or any other firm, white fish
1½ tbsp lemon juice
1 tsp salt
2.5cm/1in piece of cinnamon stick, broken up
seeds of 6 green cardamom pods
1 tsp cumin seeds
2 tsp coriander seeds
1 tbsp white poppy seeds
1 tbsp sesame seeds
4 tbsp sunflower oil or olive oil
1 large onion, finely chopped
2 tsp garlic purée
2 tsp ginger purée
½–1 tsp chilli powder
½ tsp ground turmeric
115g/4oz/½ cup thick set natural (plain) yogurt, whisked
2 medium tomatoes, sliced
2–3 tbsp chopped coriander (cilantro) leaves

1 Cut the fillets into 5cm/2in pieces and sprinkle with the lemon juice and half the salt. Rub in gently and set aside for 20 minutes to absorb the flavours. Preheat the oven to 160°C/325°F/Gas Mark 3. Grind the cinnamon, cardamom seeds, cumin, coriander, poppy and sesame seeds in a coffee grinder until finely ground. Set aside.

2 In a small pan, heat the oil over a medium heat and add the onion. Fry until it is soft and translucent, but not brown. Add the garlic and ginger, continue to fry for 2 minutes, then add the ground ingredients, chilli powder and turmeric. Cook, stirring constantly, for 1 minute, then and add the remaining salt and yogurt. Mix thoroughly and remove from the heat.

3 In a roasting pan (15cm x 30cm/6in x 12in), spread half the spice mixture, half the tomatoes and half the chopped coriander. Arrange the fish on top in a single layer. Carefully spread the remaining spice mix, chopped coriander and tomatoes over the fish. Cover the pan with a piece of foil, sealing the edges completely. Bake in the centre of the oven for 35–40 minutes.

4 Transfer to a dish and strain the juices over.

PER PORTION Energy 353kcal/1473kJ; Protein 36.2g; Carbohydrate 17.8g, of which sugars 10.6g; Fat 15.9g, of which saturates 2.3g; Cholesterol 0.2mg; Calcium 320mg; Fibre 2.2g; Sodium 126mg.

Prawn Korma

Jhinge ka Korma

This luscious recipe comes from Bhopal, the capital of the central provinces, which is well known for its fabulous fish and shellfish dishes. Raw king prawns are ideal here, but you can also use large peeled and cooked prawns if you wish, provided that they are simply heated through in the sauce and not overcooked. The almonds and yogurt, along with poppy and sesame seeds, contrast with the hot chilli, garlic and ginger to add a cooling dimension.

Serves 4

50g/2oz/½ cup blanched almonds
500g/1¼lb raw peeled king prawns (jumbo shrimp)
2 tbsp lemon juice
½ tsp ground turmeric
1 tbsp white poppy seeds
1 tbsp sesame seeds
150g/5oz/⅔ cup whole milk natural (plain) yogurt
1½ tsp gram flour
4 tbsp sunflower oil or olive oil
1 large onion, finely chopped
2 tsp ginger purée
2 tsp garlic purée
1 chilli, seeded and finely chopped
¼-½ tsp chilli powder
1 tsp salt, or to taste
1 tbsp toasted flaked (sliced) almonds, to garnish

1 Soak the almonds in 150ml/5fl oz/⅔ cup boiling water for 20 minutes.

2 In a large mixing bowl, mix the prawns, lemon juice and turmeric together. Set aside.

3 Grind the poppy and sesame seeds in a coffee grinder or blender until they are finely ground, about the consistency of salt.

4 Whisk the yogurt and gram flour together and set aside.

5 In a heavy pan, heat the oil over a medium heat and add the onion. Fry gently until the onion is soft and translucent, around 5–6 minutes.

6 Add the ginger and garlic, the ground poppy and sesame seeds, and the chilli powder. Cook for 2–3 minutes, stirring constantly, then add the prawns, salt and the whisked yogurt. Reduce the heat to low, cover the pan and cook for another 3–4 minutes.

7 Meanwhile, purée the almonds with the water in which they were soaked in a food processor or blender, and then add this to the prawns. Stir to mix well and cook for a further 5–6 minutes or until the prawns have curled up at the ends.

8 Transfer to a serving dish and garnish with the toasted almonds. This dish goes well with Basmati Rice with Caramelized Sugar.

PER PORTION Energy 143kcal/601kJ; Protein 20.4g; Carbohydrate 5.4g, of which sugars 2.7g; Fat 4.8g, of which saturates 0.7g; Cholesterol 195mg; Calcium 168mg; Fibre 0.6g; Sodium 230mg.

Chicken in Golden Saffron Sauce

Murgh Kalia Kesari

The origins of this recipe go back to the Mughal era and the ingredients used certainly evoke a time of wealth and luxury. Saffron is said to be worth its weight in gold, and its characteristic bouquet adds a unique aroma and flavour to this succulent dish. Here, the chicken is cooked in milk and the sauce is enriched with freshly made almond purée and steeped in a mouthwatering melange of cardamom, cloves and cinnamon.

Serves 4

- 50g/2oz blanched almonds
- 675g/1½lb boned chicken thighs or breast fillets, skinned and cut into 5cm/2in cubes
- 2 tsp garlic purée
- 2 tsp ginger purée
- 1 tsp ground cumin
- 1½ tsp ground coriander
- ½–1 tsp crushed dried chillies
- 1 large onion, finely chopped
- 75g/3oz/⅓ cup whole-milk natural (plain) yogurt
- 2 tsp gram flour
- 4 whole cloves
- 4 green cardamom pods, split at the top of each pod
- 2.5cm/1in piece of cinnamon stick
- 25g/1oz ghee or unsalted butter
- 300ml/½ pint/1¼ cups full cream (whole) milk
- ½ tsp saffron strands, pounded and soaked in 1 tbsp hot milk
- ½ tsp garam masala
- 1–2 fresh green chillies, seeded and cut into julienne strips, to garnish
- naan bread, to serve

1 Soak the almonds in 150ml/5fl oz/⅔ cup boiling water and set aside for 20 minutes.

2 Put the chicken, garlic, ginger, cumin, coriander, crushed chillies and onion in a heavy pan. Beat the yogurt and gram flour together and add to the pan.

3 Add the cloves, cardamom pods and cinnamon, and place the pan over a medium heat. Stir until the contents begin to sizzle. Reduce the heat to low, cover the pan and cook the chicken in its own juices for 20–25 minutes, stirring occasionally.

4 Remove the lid and increase the heat from medium to high. Cook until the liquid is reduced to a thick batter-like consistency, stirring frequently.

5 Add the ghee or butter and stir-fry the chicken for an additional 3–4 minutes, or until the fat rises to the surface of the mixture.

6 Purée the almonds with the water in which they were soaked and add to the pan. Add the milk, along with the saffron and the hot milk in which it was soaked. Stir and bring it to the boil. Reduce the heat to low and simmer, uncovered, for 5–6 minutes.

7 Add the garam masala and remove from the heat. Transfer to a serving dish and garnish with the julienne strips of green chilli. Serve immediately with pieces of naan.

PER PORTION Energy 554kcal/2321kJ; Protein 75.6g; Carbohydrate 5.1g, of which sugars 4.7g; Fat 25.9g, of which saturates 12.2g; Cholesterol 255mg; Calcium 146mg; Fibre 0.8g; Sodium 792mg.

Royal-style Chicken Korma

Murgh Korma Shahi

The presence of royal households in central India established the practice of preparing rich and luxurious food that is now widespread. There are many types of korma – and contrary to popular belief, a korma is not a dish, but a technique applied to Indian cooking. With its savoury cashew sauce, this korma recipe is different in taste to the Hyderabadi Murgh Korma from south India, even though both recipes originate from the royal kitchens.

1 Put the chicken in a large mixing bowl. Beat the yogurt and the gram flour together and add to the chicken. Add the salt, ginger and garlic, and mix thoroughly. Cover and leave in the dish to marinate for about an hour or so.

2 Heat the ghee or butter in a heavy-based pan over a medium heat and add the cinnamon, followed by the onion. Stir-fry for 5–6 minutes until the onion is soft and translucent.

3 Add the turmeric, coriander and chilli powder, stir-fry for 1 minute, then place the marinated chicken into the pan.

4 Increase the heat slightly and stir-fry the ingredients for about 3–4 minutes until the chicken changes colour.

5 Pour in 300ml/½ pint/1¼ cups warm water, bring it to the boil, reduce the heat to low, cover and simmer for 15 minutes.

6 Drain the cashew nuts and purée them in a food processor or blender with the cream. Add the cashew nut purée to the chicken and simmer for 2–3 minutes.

7 Stir in the ground cardamom and mace, remove from the heat. Served with flat bread, this dish makes a perfect al fresco summer lunch.

Serves 4

675g/1½lb boned chicken thighs or breast fillets, skinned and cut into 5cm/2in pieces
75g/3oz/⅓ cup whole milk natural (plain) yogurt
2 tsp gram flour
1 tsp salt
2 tsp ginger purée
2 tsp garlic purée
4 tbsp ghee or unsalted (sweet) butter
2.5cm/1in piece of cinnamon stick
1 large onion, finely sliced
½ tsp ground turmeric
1 tbsp ground coriander
½ tsp chilli powder, or to taste
50g/2oz/½ cup raw unsalted cashew nuts, soaked in boiling water for 15 minutes
150ml/5fl oz/⅔ cup double (heavy) cream
½ tsp ground cardamom
½ tsp ground mace

Cook's Tip

Removing the skin and any visible fat from the chicken makes a healthier dish which is lower in fat.

PER PORTION Energy 343kcal/1450kJ; Protein 54g; Carbohydrate 18g, of which sugars 10.7g; Fat 6.8g, of which saturates 2.6g; Cholesterol 151mg; Calcium 66mg; Fibre 1.8g; Sodium 197mg.

Lamb in Mango-flavoured Sauce

Aam ka Gosht

This recipe has a pleasant sweet-and-sour taste combined with the heady bouquet of spices. Lamb cooked with mango is a Mughal delicacy, and here, mangoes are cooked in a fragrant sugar syrup before they are added to the meat. As fresh mangoes can sometimes be difficult to find out of season, this recipe calls for dried, ready-to-eat mangoes, which are available all year round from supermarkets and health-food stores.

Serves 4

675g/1½lb boned leg of lamb
4 tbsp sunflower oil or olive oil
1 large onion, finely chopped
2 tsp ginger purée
2 tsp garlic purée
1 tsp ground turmeric
2 tsp ground cumin
½–1 tsp chilli powder
50g/2oz/¼ cup thick set natural (plain) yogurt
2 tsp gram flour
1 tsp salt, or to taste
2 firm, ripe tomatoes, skinned and chopped
115g/4oz dried ready-to-eat mango
½ tsp garam masala
1½ tbsp red wine vinegar
2 tbsp chopped coriander (cilantro) leaves
naan bread, to serve

1 Remove all visible fat from the meat, then cut into 5cm/2in cubes and set aside.

2 In a heavy pan, heat the oil over a medium heat and add the onion. Fry for 3–4 minutes, stirring constantly, then add the ginger and garlic.

3 Continue to fry the ginger and garlic for a further 3–4 minutes, then add the turmeric, cumin and chilli powder. Stir-fry for 30 seconds and add 3 tbsp water. Stir-fry until the water has evaporated and repeat this process twice more.

4 Add the meat to the pan and reduce the heat to low. Whisk the yogurt and the gram flour together, and then add this mixture to the meat. Blend thoroughly, cover the pan and cook for around 40–45 minutes.

5 Add the salt, tomatoes and mango. Simmer, uncovered, for 10–12 minutes, or until the sauce has thickened to a good 'gravy-like' consistency.

6 Stir in the garam masala, vinegar and half of the chopped coriander. Serve in bowls and garnish with the remaining chopped coriander. Naan bread of any variety makes an ideal accompaniment to this dish.

PER PORTION Energy 534kcal/2230kJ; Protein 38.8g; Carbohydrate 23.6g, of which sugars 17g; Fat 32.6g, of which saturates 10.8g; Cholesterol 133mg; Calcium 98mg; Fibre 3.8g; Sodium 176mg.

Saffron-scented Basmati Rice with Fragrant Lamb Curry

Biryani Khaiberi

Hailing from Afghanistan, this superb biryani dish features lamb cooked in a fragrant sauce with saffron-scented rice. The meat and rice are part-cooked, then combined in layers and baked in a tightly sealed pan in the oven, creating an irresistible flavour and texture.

Serves 4–5

675g/1½lb boned leg of lamb, cut into 2.5cm/1in cubes
50g/2oz/¼ cup thick set natural (plain) yogurt, whisked
1 tsp salt
75g/3oz ghee or unsalted (sweet) butter
2 large onions, finely sliced
2 tsp ginger purée
2 tsp garlic purée

For the ground spice mix:
2 tsp coriander seeds, finely ground
1 tsp cumin seeds, finely ground
2.5cm/1in piece of cinnamon stick, broken up and finely ground
4 cardamom pods, finely ground
4 cloves, finely ground
1 tbsp white poppy seeds, finely ground
¼ of a whole nutmeg, crushed and ground

For the rice:
½ tsp saffron strands, pounded
2 tbsp hot milk
2.5cm/1in piece of cinnamon stick
4 cardamom pods, bruised
4 cloves
2 star anise
2 whole bay leaves
2 tsp salt, or to taste
350g/12oz/1¾ cups basmati rice, washed and drained
1 tbsp ghee or unsalted butter, melted

1 Put the lamb in a large bowl. Add the yogurt and salt. Mix, and set aside for 20–30 minutes.

2 Melt the ghee over a medium heat and add the onion. Fry, stirring, until the onion is well browned. Turn off the heat and remove the onion. Drain on absorbent kitchen paper.

3 Return the pan to the heat and add the ginger and garlic, fry over a low heat for 1 minute. Add the ground spice mix and stir-fry for 1–2 minutes. Add the lamb. Stir and cook over medium heat for 2–3 minutes, then remove from the heat and set aside.

4 For the rice, soak the saffron in the hot milk and set aside. Preheat the oven to 160°C/325°F/Gas Mark 3. To part-cook the rice, boil 1.5 litres/2½ pints/6¼ cups water in a large pan and add the cinnamon, cardamom, cloves, star anise, bay leaves, salt and rice, and all the remaining ingredients except the melted ghee. Boil steadily for 2–3 minutes, then drain the rice, reserving the whole spices.

5 Spread the lamb evenly in a heavy, ovenproof pan. Top with half the fried onion and pile the rice on top, with the whole spices. Sprinkle the saffron milk and melted ghee over the top.

6 Soak a large piece of baking parchment and a towel in water, squeeze out. Place the paper on the rice and the towel on top. Seal the pan with a double thickness of foil and cover with the lid. Cook in the centre of the oven for 1 hour. Switch off the oven and leave the pan inside for 30 minutes.

7 Remove the pan from the oven and stir the biryani with a metal spoon to mix the rice and meat together. Transfer the biryani to a serving dish and garnish with the reserved fried onion.

PER PORTION Energy 769kcal/3208kJ; Protein 43.6g; Carbohydrate 67.6g, of which sugars 14.5g; Fat 36.2g, of which saturates 15g; Cholesterol 142mg; Calcium 134mg; Fibre 2.6g; Sodium 252mg.

Serves 4

8 firm, medium tomatoes
1 tbsp sunflower oil or olive oil
½ tsp cumin seeds
1cm/½in cube of fresh, finely grated root ginger
1–2 green chillies, finely chopped, and seeded if you prefer
1 tbsp raw pistachio nuts
1 tbsp seedless raisins
¼ tsp ground turmeric
½ tsp ground cumin
115g/4oz paneer, grated, or halloumi cheese, crumbled
½ tsp salt, or to taste
2 tbsp double (heavy) cream
2–3 tbsp coriander (cilantro) leaves, finely chopped

Tomatoes Stuffed with Paneer, Raisins and Pistachio

Tamatar ka Dulma

These stuffed tomatoes are delicious hot or cold. The stuffing is made from grated paneer, spiced with cumin, chilli and coriander, while raisins and pistachio nuts provide a varied texture and taste. Garden peas may be used instead of pistachios.

1 Slice off the tops of the tomatoes and scoop out the seeds and pulp. Keep the sliced tops.

2 Preheat the oven to 190°C/375°F/Gas Mark 5. In a small pan, heat the oil over a medium heat and add the cumin seeds. Fry them gently for 15–20 seconds, then add the ginger and chillies. Fry these for 1 minute and then add the pistachio nuts, raisins, turmeric and ground cumin. Cook for 1–2 minutes, then add all the remaining ingredients. Mix well with a wooden spoon and remove from the heat.

3 Divide the above mixture equally between the tomatoes and fill up the cavities. Place the reserved slices on top and arrange the tomatoes on a greased roasting pan. Place a piece of strong foil over them and seal the roasting pan completely by folding the edges of the foil all the way around the pan.

4 Bake in the centre of the oven for 15 minutes. This dish is a fabulous accompaniment to Potatoes in Mustard Oil with Toasted Sesame Seeds.

PER PORTION Energy 167kcal/700kJ; Protein 6.8g; Carbohydrate 12g, of which sugars 10.6g; Fat 11.1g, of which saturates 3.8g; Cholesterol 13.2mg; Calcium 52.3mg; Fibre 2.6g; Sodium 151mg.

Cauliflower and Green Peas in Mustard Oil

Gobi Mattar

Ghee and mustard oil are the two fats most commonly used in central India. Called 'the heart of India', this region draws influences from all over the country. In this tasty side dish, cauliflower florets and green peas are cooked in their own juices in a nutty mustard oil that is perfumed with cumin and coriander seeds.

1 Divide the cauliflower into 1cm/½in diameter florets and blanch for 3 minutes in boiling water. Plunge them in cold water to prevent further cooking.

2 Heat the oil in a large pan over a medium to high heat until smoking. Remove from the heat and add the mustard seeds, followed by the cumin, dried chilli and fenugreek seeds. Immediately follow with the green chillies and ginger. Fry, stirring, off the heat, for about a minute, then stir in the turmeric and coriander and return the pan to the heat.

3 Drain the cauliflower and add it to the pan. Add the peas and salt, then stir over a medium heat for 5–6 minutes until the cauliflower is heated through and the peas are cooked .

4 Remove from the heat and serve as an accompaniment to any lentil dish, Chicken with Stir-fried Onions and Shallots or Lamb Curry with Tomato Sauce.

Serves 4

1 large cauliflower, about 500g/1¼lb with outer leaves and stalks removed
2–3 tbsp mustard oil
½ tsp black mustard seeds
½ tsp cumin seeds
1 dried red chilli, torn into pieces
5–6 fenugreek seeds
1–2 green chillies, sliced at an angle and seeded if you prefer
2 tsp ginger purée
½ tsp ground turmeric
1 tsp ground coriander
175g/6oz frozen garden peas
½ tsp salt, or to taste

PER PORTION Energy 164kcal/678kJ; Protein 8.1g; Carbohydrate 10g, of which sugars 4.1g; Fat 10.5g, of which saturates 1.3g; Cholesterol 0mg; Calcium 42.3mg; Fibre 4.3g; Sodium 13mg.

Potatoes in Mustard Oil with Toasted Sesame Seeds

Til-Aloo

What could be more appetizing than crunchy potato cubes cooked in pungent mustard oil and topped with roasted, ground spices? To finish this splendid side dish, the tops of the potatoes are sprinkled with mustard, nigella and sesame seeds after frying, and then dusted with turmeric to create a golden tasty glow.

Serves 4

1 tsp coriander seeds
1 tsp cumin seeds
2–3 dried red chillies, torn into pieces
2 tbsp sesame seeds
800g/1¾lb potatoes
300ml/10fl oz/1¼ cups warm water
4 tbsp mustard oil
1 tsp ground turmeric
1 tsp salt, or to taste

1 In a small heavy pan, dry-roast the coriander, cumin and chillies over a medium heat for no more than 1 minute until they release their aroma. Remove to a plate and cool.

2 Return the pan to the heat and dry-roast the sesame seeds, stirring, until they go just a shade darker. Remove and allow them to cool.

3 Put the roasted spices in a coffee grinder or blender, and add all but 1 tsp of the roasted sesame seeds, reserving 1 tsp to garnish. Grind them finely and set aside.

4 Wash the potatoes and dry them with a clean cloth. Quarter or halve them according to their size so that they are all of a similar weight. Place in a pan and add 300ml/10fl oz/1¼ cups warm water and add the salt. Bring it to the boil, reduce the heat to low and cover the pan. Simmer for 12–15 minutes or until the potatoes are tender and have absorbed all the liquid.

5 In a non-stick wok or frying pan, heat the oil over a medium to high heat until smoking. Fry the potatoes in two batches until they are well browned and a crust has formed on the surface. Drain well on absorbent kitchen paper.

6 Reduce the heat to low, stir in the turmeric and quickly follow it with all the fried potatoes. Add the ground spices.

7 Transfer the potatoes to a serving dish and sprinkle the reserved sesame seeds on top. Try this as an accompaniment to Rainbow Trout in Lemon and Mustard Marinade.

PER PORTION Energy 286kcal/1196kJ; Protein 5.1g; Carbohydrate 31.6g, of which sugars 2.5g; Fat 16.4g, of which saturates 2g; Cholesterol 0mg; Calcium 68.2mg; Fibre 2.5g; Sodium 24mg.

Cumin and Saffron-scented Wholemeal Flat Bread

Bhopali Roti

This is a rich bread with a superb taste and flavour that does not need to be supported by a spicy curry – its attractive appearance and fresh blend of spices make it good enough to eat on its own. Cumin and saffron are the key ingredients, but the addition of fresh chillies and coriander make it even more aromatic.

1 Soak the cashews and saffron together in 100ml/3½fl oz/scant ½ cup boiling water for 15 minutes. Dry-roast the cumin seeds in a small heavy pan for a minute. Remove the nuts and seeds from the pan, cool and crush in a mortar and pestle. In a mixing bowl, mix the chapati flour, ground rice, salt, chilli, coriander and crushed cumin together. Rub in the ghee or butter.

2 Purée the cashew nuts and saffron with their soaking water in a blender, add this to the flour. Mix with fingertips and gradually add 120ml/4fl oz/½ cup warm water. Mix until a dough is formed, and knead for 4–5 minutes until pliable. Cover with a cloth and rest for 30 minutes.

3 Divide into 12 balls, rotate between the palms to make them smooth. Flatten each into a round cake 1cm/½in thick. Dust with flour and roll out to a 15cm/6in disc. Preheat a heavy griddle and place a cake on it. Cook for 2 minutes and turn over. Spread 1 tsp oil on surface and turn it over. Cook for 2 minutes until browned. Repeat for uncooked side and other discs.

Makes 12

- 50g/2oz raw unsalted cashew nuts
- pinch of saffron
- 1 tsp cumin seeds
- 350g/12oz/3 cups chapati flour, plus extra for dusting
- 115g/4oz/⅔ cup ground rice
- ½ tsp salt
- 1 green chilli, finely chopped or minced, and seeded if you prefer
- 1 tbsp coriander (cilantro) leaves, finely chopped
- 1 tbsp ghee or unsalted (sweet) butter
- 1 tbsp sunflower oil or olive oil
- oil for shallow-frying

PER PORTION Energy 169kcal/710kJ; Protein 5.4g; Carbohydrate 27.3g, of which sugars 0.9g; Fat 4.8g, of which saturates 1.3g; Cholesterol 3mg; Calcium 15mg; Fibre 2.8g; Sodium 22mg.

Makes 16 pieces

225g/8oz raw unsalted cashew nuts
100g/3¾oz/½ cup caster (superfine) sugar
1 tbsp ghee or unsalted (sweet) butter
½ tsp ground cardamom

Baked Cashew Nut Diamonds

Kaju Burfi

An extremely popular sweet dish found all over India, these tasty cakes are made using cashew nuts and flavoured with delicate cardamom. Kaju Burfi is very simple to make: a soft dough is formed from the ground cashew nuts, caster sugar and ghee, then flattened and baked in the oven.

1 Soak the cashew nuts in boiling water for 20 minutes, drain them and then place in a food processor or blender. Blend the nuts until they make up a smooth paste, and then transfer the paste to a flat, dry surface.

2 Add the remaining ingredients and knead the mixture carefully, until it becomes smooth and buttery in texture.

3 Preheat the oven to 160°C/325°F/Gas Mark 3. Line a baking sheet with a well-greased baking parchment and spread the mixture on it to form a 20cm/8in square. Bake in the centre of the oven for 35–40 minutes until lightly browned.

4 Remove the cashew dish from the oven and allow it cool to 15 minutes, then cut into diamonds or squares. This is delicious served at tea time or after dinner with coffee or tea.

PER PORTION Energy 117kcal/490kJ; Protein 2.9g; Carbohydrate 9.2g, of which sugars 7.3g; Fat 7.9g, of which saturates 1.9g; Cholesterol 2mg; Calcium 8mg; Fibre 0.5g; Sodium 48mg.

west india

Fertile land and plentiful supplies of vegetables, seafood and dairy produce promote a delightful and varied cuisine, from Goan Prawn Curry and Crab in Roasted Coconut Sauce to Sweet Peppers with Whole Cashew Nuts and Spicy Stuffed Bananas.

West India

Four states of varying sizes make up the region of West India: Goa, a tiny enclave perched on the west coast; Maharashtra, a large state stretching from the Arabian Sea across almost the whole width of India; Gujarat, another coastal state that proudly claims to be the birthplace of many of India's political leaders, including Gandhi; and finally Rajasthan, a vast landlocked desert region bordering Pakistan.

Rajasthan is the ancient land of Indian emperors and princes, where a suitably elaborate cuisine was developed for these royal personages to enjoy, often using the game caught during a day's hunting. Despite the royal culinary tradition, there are many vegetarians in this state, including most members of the Marwari community, the main controllers of business and finance whose influence has spread throughout India.

Within the colourful diversity of Indian regional cuisine, Gujarat merits a special position of pride as the state that has perfected the true art of vegetarian cooking, mainly owing to the strong influence of the Jain religion. Gujarati cooks have not found this particularly restricting and have created a dazzling array of delicious and nutritious dishes that have become famous across the whole of India. The three main regions of Gujarat have distinct climatic differences, which have led to a very varied cuisine. Western Gujarat is an arid area where there is a scarcity of fresh vegetables, but it is rich in dairy produce, and there is a strong tradition of making delicious sweetmeats and desserts based on milk and yogurt. Central Gujarat is known as the 'granary of Gujarat' because of its abundance of grain crops. The south of the state, with a much wetter climate, is covered with lush green vegetation, and here a fantastic variety of fresh vegetables grow.

The food of the large state of Maharashtra is fiery, as both chillies and black pepper are used with great relish. Peanuts and cashew nuts are another distinctive feature of Maharashtrian cooking, and peanut oil is the basis of many dishes. The people here have a sweet tooth, and use a lot of palm sugar (jaggery) and kokum, a purple berry-like fruit with a pleasant sweet-and-sour taste. Mumbai (Bombay), the capital of Maharashtra, is a historic and cosmopolitan city, also known as the Gateway of India. Here all sorts of dishes have been created by the different communities that have made Mumbai their home – it is a real food-lover's paradise. It is probably the only city in India where you can sample food from almost anywhere in the country, as well as recipes that owe much to foreign influences. The latest invasion in Mumbai is from the Bollywood film industry, helping to maintain a high level of excitement and artistic passion in the city.

The tiny state of Goa, on the southern edge of West India, was ruled, in turn, by Hindus, Muslims, Portuguese Christians and the British. The lure of Indian spices and silks brought the Portuguese explorer Vasco da Gama to this part of India, and the Portuguese established an eastern empire for themselves with Goa as the central state. Although local ingredients such as fish and coconut predominate, Goa's cuisine also reflects the influence of European culture, for example the term vindaloo originally derived from the Portuguese words for 'vinegar' and 'garlic'.

Spicy Scrambled Eggs

Akoori

If you want a breakfast that really wakes you up in the morning, these spicy scrambled eggs are ideal. Served with Indian bread or toast with lashings of butter, they are delicious. They can also be served as a topping for canapés at drinks parties, where they go wonderfully well with chilled white or rosé wine. This recipe comes from a small group of people in western India, known as the Parsees, whose name reflects their Persian origins.

Serves 4

3 tbsp sunflower oil or olive oil
1 large onion, finely chopped
1–2 green chillies, finely chopped
1 tsp grated fresh root ginger (optional)
⅓ tsp ground turmeric
2 salad tomatoes, finely chopped
1 tbsp chopped fresh coriander (cilantro) leaves
½ tsp salt, or to taste
4 large eggs, whisked
toast or Indian bread, to serve

1 Heat the oil in a frying pan over a medium heat and add the onion, green chillies and ginger, if using. Stir-fry for 5–6 minutes until the onion is soft.

2 Add the turmeric and tomatoes, cook for 1 minute and add the coriander and salt.

3 Add the eggs to the pan and whisk until they reach the desired consistency. Indian scrambled eggs are usually made slightly drier than the Western version, but if you prefer creamier eggs, add a tablespoon of full-fat (whole) milk.

4 Transfer to plates and serve accompanied by one of the Indian breads featured in this book, or alternatively, try crunchy toast and butter.

PER PORTION Energy 203kcal/843kJ; Protein 8.4g; Carbohydrate 10.8g, of which sugars 7.2g; Fat 14.6g, of which saturates 2.7g; Cholesterol 190mg; Calcium 64mg; Fibre 1.9g; Sodium 79mg.

Makes 12

- 2 slices of white bread, a day or two old
- 400g/14oz cooked peeled prawns (shrimp)
- 3 tbsp sunflower oil or olive oil
- 1 tsp fennel seeds
- 1 large onion, finely chopped
- 2 green chillies, finely chopped (seeded if preferred)
- 2 tsp ginger purée
- ½ tsp garam masala
- 2 tbsp chopped coriander (cilantro) leaves
- salt to taste
- 25g/1oz/¼ cup plain (all-purpose) flour
- 1 egg, beaten
- 75g/3oz/1½ cups golden breadcrumbs
- oil for deep-frying
- salad and lemon wedges, to garnish

PER PORTION Energy 165kcal/688kJ; Protein 8.1g; Carbohydrate 11.2g, of which sugars 2.2g; Fat 10.1g, of which saturates 1.2g; Cholesterol 81mg; Calcium 53mg; Fibre 0.7g; Sodium 139mg.

Prawn Rissoles

Rissóis de Camrao

This is a Portuguese-influenced dish from Goa, where seafood is caught fresh and cooked fresh on a daily basis. Small frozen prawns are ideal for this recipe, since they will be chopped and blended with a selection of pungent spices.

1 Soak the bread in cold water and drain. Place it in a food processor and blend until it is smooth. Add the prawns and, using the pulse action, chop them coarsely. Remove and place the mixture into a medium-sized mixing bowl.

2 Heat the oil in a small pan over a medium heat and add fennel seeds. Stir-fry for 30 seconds. Add the onion, chilli and ginger. Continue stir-frying until the mixture begins to brown, then add the garam masala. Add this mixture to the prawns, then add the chopped coriander and salt to taste. Mix the ingredients thoroughly, cover the bowl and chill for 30–40 minutes.

3 Divide the prawn mixture into 12 equal portions and form them into rissoles. Dust each rissole in the flour, dip in the egg and roll in the breadcrumbs.

4 Heat the oil in a wok and deep-fry the rissoles over a medium to high heat in small batches until they are crisp and golden brown. Drain well on kitchen paper and serve with a salad garnish of cucumber and tomatoes, and wedges of lemon.

Goan Prawn Curry

Camrao de Caldeen

Perhaps it is no surprise that an exquisite seafood cuisine has developed in Goa – this area of India is resplendent with flourishing rice fields, coconut palms and clusters of cashew trees, on a vast coastline that yields a steady harvest of fish and shellfish. Goan dishes use generous amounts of chilli, mellowed by coconut milk and palm vinegar. In this delicious coconut-enriched prawn curry, cider vinegar makes an equally good alternative to palm vinegar.

Serves 4

500g/1¼lb peeled king or tiger prawns (jumbo shrimp)
½ tsp salt, plus extra to taste
2 tbsp palm or cider vinegar
4 tbsp sunflower oil or olive oil
1 large onion, finely chopped
2 tsp ginger purée
2 tsp garlic purée
½ tsp ground cumin
1 tsp ground coriander
½ tsp ground turmeric
½ tsp chilli powder
½ tsp ground black pepper
75g/3oz/1 cup creamed coconut, cut into small pieces (or 1 cup coconut cream)
4 green chillies, left whole on the stalks
2 tbsp chopped fresh coriander (cilantro) leaves
plain boiled rice, to serve

1 Put the prawns in a non-metallic bowl and add the measured salt and vinegar. Mix together well and set aside for about 10–15 minutes.

2 Heat the sunflower or olive oil in a medium-sized pan and add the onion. Fry over a medium heat until the onion is translucent.

3 Add the ginger and garlic and continue to fry for about 2 minutes over a low heat, being careful to lightly brown, but not burn, the ingredients.

4 Mix the cumin, coriander, turmeric, chilli powder and black pepper in a bowl and add 2 tbsp water to make a good pouring consistency.

5 Add this mixture to the onion and cook, stirring, for 4–5 minutes until the mixture is dry and the oil separates from the spice mix.

6 Next, pour in 200ml/7fl oz/¾ cup warm water, the creamed coconut and salt to taste, if desired. Stir over a medium heat until the coconut has dissolved.

7 Add the prawns along with all the juices in the bowl, bring the pan to the boil, reduce the heat and cook for another 5–7 minutes. When the prawns curl up, they are cooked.

8 Add the fresh chillies and simmer for an additional 2–3 minutes. Stir in the chopped coriander, remove from the heat and serve with plain boiled rice.

PER PORTION Energy 171kcal/723kJ; Protein 21.9g; Carbohydrate 10g, of which sugars 7.4g; Fat 5.3g, of which saturates 2.5g; Cholesterol 227mg; Calcium 136mg; Fibre 1g; Sodium 344mg.

Crab in Roasted Coconut Sauce

Crab Xec Xec

Serves 4

- 2 large fresh uncooked crabs, about 400g/14oz each
- 75g/3oz/1 cup desiccated (dry unsweetened shredded) coconut
- 3 cloves
- 10 black peppercorns
- 5–6 dried red chillies
- 1 tbsp coriander seeds
- 1 tsp cumin seeds
- 3 tbsp sunflower oil or plain olive oil
- 1 large onion, finely chopped
- 1 tsp ginger purée
- 1 tsp garlic purée
- 1–2 green chillies, finely chopped (seeded if preferred)
- ½ tsp ground turmeric
- ¾ tsp salt, or to taste
- 1½ tbsp tamarind juice or lime juice
- plain boiled basmati rice, to serve

Cook's Tip

Fresh crabs are available all year round, but they are at their best from the months of April through to December.

PER PORTION Energy 295kcal/1223kJ; Protein 11.4g; Carbohydrate 11.7g, of which sugars 6.8g; Fat 23.1g, of which saturates 11.2g; Cholesterol 22mg; Calcium 55mg; Fibre 4g; Sodium 648mg.

For this recipe, fresh crabs, cut into pieces, are simmered gently in a spice-laced roasted coconut sauce, which is then served with plain boiled rice. For those who don't fancy preparing live crabs, frozen crab claws may be used, or alternatively, pre-prepared crabs, along with all the juices. This is a hot curry, but you can adjust the level of pungency to taste by reducing the amount of green chillies.

1 To prepare a fresh uncooked crab: lay the crab on its back and remove the claws and legs with a twisting action, and then remove the feathery toes. Pull the centre portion from the main shell and remove the stomach sac, gills and lungs. Extract the meat, wash the shell and reserve. This will add flavour to the sauce. Some people discard the toes, but these will add extra flavour to the dish and they do have a little meat inside the shell. Finally, wash the claws, legs and toes and reserve.

2 In a small heavy pan or frying pan, dry-roast the coconut over a low heat, stirring constantly until the coconut is lightly browned. Do not allow it to darken too much. Remove the coconut and wipe clean the pan clean.

3 Next, dry-roast the cloves, peppercorns, dried red chillies, coriander and cumin seeds for about 1 minute until they release their aroma. Remove and allow to cool.

4 Grind the roasted coconut and the spices in a coffee grinder or blender, in small batches if necessary, and set aside. Heat the oil over a medium heat and fry the onion, ginger, garlic and green chillies for 8–10 minutes or until the mixture is just beginning to brown.

5 Stir in the turmeric, crab pieces (including the reserved shell but not the extracted meat) and salt. Pour in 350ml/12fl oz/1½ cups warm water and add the ground spices. Cook gently for 3–4 minutes, then add the reserved crab meat.

6 Cook for a further 2–3 minutes, then add the tamarind juice or lime juice. Stir and cook for about 1 minute and remove from the heat. Serve with plain boiled basmati rice.

Hot Chicken Curry from Kolhapur

Murgh Kolhapuri

This very hot curry comes from the small town of Kolhapur, in the state of Maharashtra. Large amounts of chillies as well as hot spices such as cloves and peppercorns are used, but the final taste is balanced by the sweetness of a generous amount of onion, yogurt and coconut. For a milder taste, reduce the amount of chillies, peppercorns and cloves or add extra coconut and yogurt.

Serves 4

- 1.1kg/2½lb chicken joints
- 115g/4oz/½ cup natural (plain) yogurt
- 2 tsp gram flour
- 1 tsp ground turmeric
- 1 tsp salt or to taste
- 25g/1oz/⅓ cup desiccated (dry unsweetened shredded) coconut
- 1 large onion, roughly chopped
- 2.5cm/1in piece of fresh root ginger, chopped
- 5 large garlic cloves, roughly chopped
- 4 tbsp sunflower oil or olive oil
- 5cm/2in piece of cinnamon stick, halved
- 6 green cardamom pods, bruised
- 6 cloves
- 1–2 tsp chilli powder
- ½ tsp ground black pepper
- 115g/4oz chopped canned tomatoes, with their juice
- ½ tsp garam masala
- 1 tbsp chopped fresh coriander (cilantro) leaves
- 1 small tomato, seeded and cut into julienne strips, to garnish
- 1–2 green chillies, seeded and cut into julienne strips, to garnish

1 Skin the chicken joints and cut each joint into two pieces by separating the leg from the thigh and cutting each breast joint in half.

2 In a large mixing bowl, whisk the yogurt with the gram flour, then add the turmeric and salt. Add the chicken pieces and mix thoroughly. Set aside for 1 hour.

3 In a heavy pan, dry-roast the coconut over a medium to low heat until it is lightly browned. Do not allow it to darken. Remove the coconut from the pan, cool and grind in a coffee grinder or blender until fine. Purée the onion, ginger and garlic in a food processor or blender until smooth.

4 Heat the oil over a low heat and add the cinnamon, cardamom and cloves. Stir-fry these until the cardamom pods have puffed up, then add the puréed onion, ginger and garlic mixture gradually. Increase the heat slightly and cook until the mixture is beginning to brown, stirring regularly and being careful not to blacken.

5 Add the chilli powder and black pepper, and continue to cook for an additional 2–3 minutes, adding about a tablespoon of water if the mixture sticks to the pan.

6 Add the chicken and stir over a high heat until it changes colour. Add the tomatoes and pour in 200ml/7fl oz/¾ cup warm water. Bring the pan to the boil, reduce the heat to low, cover the pan and cook until the chicken is tender when pierced with a fork.

7 Stir in the roasted coconut and cook for 4–5 minutes. Stir in garam masala and coriander. Remove from the heat. Transfer to a dish, garnish with tomato and chilli, and serve with rice.

PER PORTION Energy 605kcal/2508kJ; Protein 37.8g; Carbohydrate 13.8g, of which sugars 8.9g; Fat 44.7g, of which saturates 13.2g; Cholesterol 176.2mg; Calcium 107.8mg; Fibre 2.5g; Sodium 170mg.

Stuffed Quails

Batair Mussallam

Serves 4

4 quails

For the stuffing:

50g/2oz/½ cup grated paneer (Indian cheese)
15g/½oz seedless raisins
2 dried, ready-to-eat apricots, finely chopped
1 tsp ginger purée
1–2 green chillies, finely chopped
1 tbsp coriander (cilantro) leaves, chopped
¼ tsp salt
1 tbsp double (heavy) cream

For the sauce:

1 tbsp coriander seeds
2–3 dried red chillies, chopped
2 tbsp white poppy seeds
1 tbsp sesame seeds
½ mace blade
¼ tsp ground turmeric
3 tbsp sunflower oil or olive oil
4 green cardamom pods, bruised
2.5cm/1in piece of cinnamon stick
1 medium onion, finely chopped
2 tsp ginger purée
2 tsp garlic purée
115g/4oz/½ cup natural (plain) yogurt
2 tsp gram flour
naan bread or griddle-cooked flaky bread, to serve

PER PORTION Energy 378kcal/1581kJ; Protein 25g; Carbohydrate 18.8g, of which sugars 9.1g; Fat 23.6g, of which saturates 6.4g; Cholesterol 97mg; Calcium 194mg; Fibre 1.9g; Sodium 144mg.

The state of Rajasthan is largely vegetarian, but Mughal emperors were quite passionate about hunting, so their chefs created a delectable range of game dishes. This recipe follows the dictums of traditional Mughal cooking: the stomach cavity of the birds is filled with grated Indian cheese (paneer), dried apricots, chillies and spices, and the stuffed birds are gently braised in an aromatic sauce.

1 Clean the quails and wipe inside and out. To allow the quails to absorb all the flavours, score the skin, making a few incisions in the flesh at the same time.

2 Mix the stuffing ingredients and divide into four portions. Stuff the stomach cavity of each quail with this, pushing it up as far as possible. Truss the birds with toothpicks (cocktail sticks).

3 To make the sauce, process the coriander, red chillies, poppy and sesame seeds, and the mace in a coffee grinder until finely ground. Place in a bowl and mix in the turmeric, then set aside.

4 In a large heavy pan, heat the oil over a low heat and add the cardamom and cinnamon. Stir-fry until the cardamom pods have puffed up. Add the onion, ginger and garlic and fry for about 5–6 minutes until the onion is soft, stirring frequently.

5 Add ground ingredients and cook for 1 minute. Whisk yogurt and gram flour and add to the pan. Add the salt and cook for 2–3 minutes. Pour in 120ml/4fl oz/½ cup warm water and mix.

6 Add the stuffed quails and turn them around in the pan until they are coated with the spices. Now put the birds close together in the pan, breast side down. Turn the heat to very low.

7 Soak a piece of baking parchment and squeeze out the water. Place in the pan, making sure it is not touching the birds. Cover the pan tightly and cook for 20 minutes.

8 Remove the lid, turn the birds on their backs and re-cover as before with the baking parchment. Cook for 20 minutes. Prick the thighs with a fork to see if the juices are running clear; if not, cook for a few minutes longer. Serve with naan or flaky bread.

Pork in Garlic and Vinegar

Vindaloo

Vindaloo is Goa's signature dish, first introduced by Portuguese traders who took pork preserved in vinegar ('vin') and garlic ('alhoo') with them on their long voyages to India. More than just the fiery-hot taste its reputation suggests, Vindaloo presents a well-rounded, spicy and enjoyable dish that makes a superb meal served with plain boiled basmati rice or plain naan bread.

1 Soak the chillies in hot water for about 10–15 minutes until softened. Put them into a blender along with the ginger, garlic, vinegar and tamarind or lime juice. Blend the ingredients until they make up a smooth purée.

2 Grind the cumin, coriander, cloves, cinnamon, peppercorns, mace, cardamom and fenugreek seeds, bark and blade together in a coffee grinder or blender until you have a fine powder. Add this to the puréed ingredients and make a paste. Rub about a quarter of the spice paste into the meat and set aside for 30 minutes.

3 Heat the oil in a heavy pan over a medium heat and fry the onions for about 8–10 minutes until they are lightly browned, stirring frequently. Add the reserved spice paste and fry for 5–6 minutes, stirring continuously. Sprinkle in a little water from time to time to prevent the spices from sticking to the bottom of the pan.

4 Add the marinated pork and sauté for 5–6 minutes. Add the salt and sugar and pour in 250ml/8fl oz/1 cup warm water. Bring this mixture to the boil, then reduce the heat to low and simmer until the meat is tender.

5 For the flavoured oil, in a very small pan or a ladle, heat the sunflower or vegetable oil over a medium heat. When this is hot, switch off the heat source and add the curry leaves.

6 Let the curry leaves sizzle in the oil for 15–20 seconds, then stir the flavoured oil into the vindaloo meat. Serve with plain boiled basmati rice or naan bread.

Serves 4

2–6 dried red chillies
25g/1oz fresh root ginger, roughly chopped
25g/1oz cloves of garlic cloves, chopped
120ml/4fl oz/½ cup cider vinegar
1 tbsp tamarind juice or lime juice
1 tsp cumin seeds
1 tsp coriander seeds
6 cloves
5cm/2in piece of cinnamon stick, broken up
8–10 black peppercorns
1 blade of mace
seeds of 2 black cardamom pods
¼ tsp fenugreek seeds
675g/1½lb pork leg steaks, cut into 2.5cm/1 in cubes
4 tbsp oil
2 large onions, finely chopped
1 tsp salt, or to taste
1 tsp soft dark brown sugar

For the flavoured oil:

2 tsp sunflower or vegetable oil
8–10 curry leaves

PER PORTION Energy 419kcal/1728kJ; Protein 41.5g; Carbohydrate 19.4g, of which sugars 11g; Fat 19.7g, of which saturates 3.8g; Cholesterol 110.3mg; Calcium 76mg; Fibre 2.7g; Sodium 132mg.

Lamb Cooked with Lentils and Vegetables

Dhansak

Serves 4

For the lamb:

3 tbsp sunflower oil or olive oil
1 large onion, finely chopped
2 tsp ginger purée
2 tsp garlic purée
1 tsp coriander seeds
½ tsp cumin seeds
4 green cardamom pods
2.5cm/1in piece of cinnamon stick, broken
10–12 black peppercorns
2 bay leaves
5–6 fenugreek seeds
½ tsp black mustard seeds
1 tsp chilli powder or to taste
675g/1½lb boned leg of lamb, cut into 2.5cm/2in cubes
150g/5oz canned chopped tomatoes
1 tsp salt, or to taste

For the lentils and vegetables:

75g/3oz/⅓ cup each yellow split peas and red split lentils
2 tbsp sunflower oil or olive oil
1 medium onion, finely chopped
2 green chillies, chopped
1 tsp ground turmeric
1 small aubergine (eggplant), cut into 5cm/2in pieces
1 tsp salt or to taste
2 tbsp tamarind juice or lime juice
1 tbsp chopped coriander (cilantro) leaves plus extra sprigs, to garnish

PER PORTION Energy 470kcal/1970kJ; Protein 32.7g; Carbohydrate 36.5g, of which sugars 9g; Fat 22.7g, of which saturates 7.1g; Cholesterol 85.5mg; Calcium 106mg; Fibre 4.8g; Sodium 133mg.

This deliciously piquant dish originated in the state of Gujarat, where the ancient Persians first landed after fleeing from their own country (now known as Iran). Here, cubed lamb is browned and simmered with a mouthwatering medley of pungent, freshly ground spices, then brought together with separately prepared lentils and vegetables, before being served alongside basmati rice.

1 In a heavy pan, heat the oil over a medium heat and add the onion. Stir-fry until the onion is soft but not brown, then add the ginger and garlic and continue to stir-fry until the mixture begins to brown, but not smoke.

2 Grind the coriander, cumin, cardamom, cinnamon stick, peppercorns, bay leaves, fenugreek and black mustard seeds finely in a coffee grinder or blender. Add the chilli powder and ground spices to the onion mixture in the pan and cook for 2 minutes, and then add the meat. Stir-fry over a high heat until the meat changes colour. Add the tomatoes and salt, and pour in 120ml/4fl oz/½ cup warm water. Bring the pan to the boil, cover and simmer for 35–40 minutes, stirring occasionally.

3 Meanwhile, for the lentil and vegetable mixture, wash both types of lentils and drain.

4 Heat the oil in a medium-sized pan and fry the onion and green chillies over a medium heat until browned, about 8–9 minutes. Stir in the turmeric, followed by the lentils and aubergine. Reduce the heat to low and stir-fry the lentils for 1–2 minutes.

5 Pour in 600ml/1 pint/2½ cups warm water, bring to the boil, reduce the heat to low and simmer for 20–25 minutes, stirring. Stir in the salt, remove pan from heat and cool slightly, then push the lentils through a sieve (strainer). Discard any coarse mixture left in the sieve.

6 Add the tamarind or lime juice to the lentils. Pour the mixture over the lamb and simmer for 15–20 minutes longer, stirring several times to ensure the lentils do not stick to the bottom of the pan. Stir in the chopped coriander and remove from the heat. Serve garnished with the sprigs of coriander, accompanied by basmati rice.

Spicy Stuffed Bananas

Kela Na Sambhariya

This unusual vegetarian recipe from Gujarat is easy to prepare and requires very little time to cook – perfect for unexpected guests. It makes a substantial and healthy main course when teamed with a lentil dish or a vegetable curry and accompanied by basmati rice.

1 Wash bananas, then trim the ends. Slit each banana lengthways halfway through its diameter, leaving 2.5mm/⅛in uncut at each end. Slit to half its diameter and set aside.

2 In a small heavy pan, dry-roast the gram flour for 1 minute, stirring constantly, then add the cumin, coriander, and green and red chillies. Stir over a medium heat for 1 minute, remove from the heat and cool. Add the chopped coriander and salt, mix well. Divide into four portions.

3 Preheat the oven to 180°C/350°F/Gas Mark 4. Pull the slit banana apart very gently and fill the gap with a portion of the gram flour filling, packing the filling in very tightly.

4 Fill the remaining bananas, then heat the oil in a wide, shallow, ovenproof pan over a medium heat. Place stuffed bananas in the hot oil, stuffed side up, reduce heat to low, cover and cook for 2 minutes. Remove the lid and spoon some hot oil on the stuffing, pressing it down gently.

5 Transfer the bananas in their dish to the oven. Bake for 12–15 minutes, basting with the oil once or twice. Serve with plain basmati rice.

Serves 4

4 ripe, firm bananas
50g/2oz/½ cup gram flour, sifted
½ tsp ground cumin
1 tsp ground coriander
1 green chilli, finely chopped, and seeded if you prefer
1 fresh red chilli, finely chopped, and seeded if you prefer
1 tbsp chopped fresh coriander (cilantro) leaves
½ tsp salt, or to taste
4 tbsp sunflower oil or olive oil

Cook's Tip

These bananas look great when served on a banana leaf and garnished with strips of fresh red chillies. Banana leaves can be bought from all good Asian shops.

PER PORTION Energy 268kcal/1122kJ; Protein 3.1g; Carbohydrate 39.6g, of which sugars 26.3g; Fat 11.9g, of which saturates 1.5g; Cholesterol 0mg; Calcium 30mg; Fibre 1.8g; Sodium 3mg.

Serves 8

- 1 each sweet red, yellow and green (bell) pepper, about 150g/5oz each
- 200g/7oz potatoes, cut into 2.5 cm/1in cubes
- 1 tbsp each sesame and white poppy seeds
- 2 tsp yellow split lentils
- 10 black peppercorns
- 1 dried red chilli, torn into pieces
- 3 tbsp sunflower oil or olive oil
- ½ tsp each black mustard and cumin seeds
- ½ tsp ground turmeric
- 50g/2oz raw whole unsalted cashew nuts
- 1 tsp salt, or to taste
- 1½ tbsp lemon juice
- 1 tbsp soft light brown sugar

Sweet Peppers with Whole Cashew Nuts

Kairas

In this recipe, sweet peppers in red, emerald and golden colours are enrobed in a thick, rich sauce with the nutty taste of sesame and poppy seeds, the earthy taste of channa dhal and the fragrance of intense yellow turmeric. Whole cashew nuts add a crunchy bite.

1 Seed the peppers, remove the cores and discard, then cut the peppers into 2.5cm/1in cubes.

2 In a medium-sized pan, bring 300ml/10fl oz/1¼ cups water to the boil and add the potatoes. Bring back to the boil, cover the pan and cook for another 5–6 minutes or until the potatoes are tender. Remove the potatoes with a slotted spoon and spread them on a large plate to prevent further cooking. Reserve the cooking liquid.

3 Grind the sesame seeds, poppy seeds, lentils, peppercorns and chilli in a coffee grinder or blender until they are finely ground.

4 Heat the sunflower or olive oil in a pan over a medium heat, then add the mustard seeds, followed by the cumin. Add the ground ingredients, turmeric and cashew nuts. Stir-fry for 30–40 seconds before adding the peppers and salt.

5 Add the potatoes and the reserved cooking liquid, plus another 150ml/5fl oz/⅔ cup warm water. Cook for 3–4 minutes and add the lemon juice and sugar. Cook for a further 2–3 minutes until the sugar has dissolved. Serve with rice.

PER PORTION Energy 146kcal/607kJ; Protein 3.45g; Carbohydrate 9.5g, of which sugars 4g; Fat 10.8g, of which saturates 1.6g; Cholesterol 0mg; Calcium 45mg; Fibre 1.8g; Sodium 24.8mg.

Aubergine Pickle

Brinjal Achar

In this tangy pickle recipe, the most important step is preparing the aubergine carefully, as the moisture from the vegetable must be extracted completely before preserving in the spice-perfumed oil. First, the aubergine is salted and left for 6–7 hours – this process does not need your attention, simply salt the pieces and leave to drain for a few hours or even overnight. The pickle is delicious served with a range of snacks, such as poppadums, and as a condiment.

Makes 350–400g/12–14oz pickle

1 large aubergine (eggplant), approx 400g/14oz, peeled and diced
1 tbsp salt
120ml/4fl oz/½ cup vegetable oil
½ tsp ground asafoetida
10 garlic cloves, crushed
5cm/2in piece of fresh root ginger, grated
1 tsp mustard seeds
1 tsp fenugreek seeds
1½ tsp cumin seeds
25g/1oz/2 tbsp granulated (white) sugar
20g/¾oz/2 scant tbsp salt
175ml/6fl oz/¾ cup white wine vinegar

1 Cube the aubergine and then sprinkle the chunks with salt and mix well. Put them in muslin (cheesecloth), tie it up, and place in a colander over a bowl. Put a clean weight directly on top and leave to drain off all the water. This will take aproximately 6–7 hours.

2 Heat the vegetable oil over a medium heat and add the asafoetida, followed by the garlic and ginger. Stir-fry for about 1 minute.

3 Grind the mustard, fenugreek and cumin seeds finely in a coffee grinder or blender. Add the ground ingredients to the pan and fry for 2 minutes. Next, add the sugar, salt, vinegar and aubergine chunks. Stir, then simmer gently for 20–25 minutes or until the aubergine is tender. Cool completely and store in a sterilized jar. Allow 12–14 days for the pickle to mature, then serve as a condiment alongside many Indian snacks and dishes.

PER PORTION Energy 870kcal/3609kJ; Protein 9.1g; Carbohydrate 46.7g, of which sugars 34.8g; Fat 73.7g, of which saturates 8g; Cholesterol 0mg; Calcium 89mg; Fibre 9.6g; Sodium 3946mg.

Serves 4–5

275g/10oz/1⅓ cups basmati rice
4 tbsp sunflower oil or olive oil
4 tsp granulated (white) sugar
1 tsp cumin seeds
2.5cm/1in piece of cinnamon stick
4 cardamom pods, bruised
6 cloves
10 black peppercorns
1 tsp salt, or to taste

Basmati Rice with Caramelized Sugar

Peela Bhat

This rice is the traditional accompaniment for Dhansak, although its mild, slightly sweet flavour makes it ideal for serving with any other curry. To make this, the uncooked rice is briefly tossed in caramelized sugar before cooking with cumin seeds and cardamom pods.

1 Wash the rice two or three times in cold water or until the water runs clear, then soak it for about 20 minutes. Leave the rice to drain in a colander.

2 In a heavy pan, heat the oil over a medium heat and add the sugar. The sugar will begin to turn brown in a few seconds and as soon as this happens, add the whole spices and other ingredients except the salt, but do not stir. Let this sizzle for 15–20 seconds.

3 Add the rice and salt, then stir-fry for 2–3 minutes, then pour in 600ml/1 pint/2½ cups warm water. Bring the pan to the boil and let it boil steadily for 1 minute. Cover the pan tightly and reduce the heat to low. Cook for 10 minutes without lifting the lid.

4 Remove the pan from the heat and leave it undisturbed for 10 minutes.

5 Fluff up the rice with a fork and serve with a meat curry such as Lamb Cooked with Lentil and Vegetables, or a vegetable main course dish such as Vegetable Korma. It is also perfect with fish curries such as Prawn Korma.

PER PORTION Energy 324kcal/1353kJ; Protein 4.1g; Carbohydrate 56.4g, of which sugars 12.5g; Fat 9.1g, of which saturates 1.1g; Cholesterol 0mg; Calcium 17mg; Fibre 0g; Sodium 1mg.

Goan Banana Fritters

Filoss

Serves 4

1 tbsp flaked (sliced) almonds
4 large bananas
1 tbsp lemon juice
150g/5oz/1¼ cups plain (all-purpose) flour
¼ tsp ground nutmeg
½ tsp ground cardamom
½ tsp ground cinnamon
2–3 tbsp soft light brown sugar
½ tsp salt
2 medium eggs
120ml/4fl oz/½ cup milk
oil for deep-frying
1 tbsp brandy (optional)
25g/1oz apricot jam or apricot glaze
whipped cream, to serve

PER PORTION Energy 522kcal/2199kJ; Protein 9.6g; Carbohydrate 72.3g, of which sugars 40g; Fat 23.7g, of which saturates 3.3g; Cholesterol 97mg; Calcium 122mg; Fibre 2.6g; Sodium 56mg.

Banana fritters make a scrumptious dessert served with a generous dollop of fresh whipped cream – or alternatively, ice cream. Delicately spiced with nutmeg and cinnamon, every mouthful of these fritters will delight the palate with its wonderful mixture of varied textures. Their sweetness and smooth finish provide the perfect finale for a meal that has featured a spicy hot main dish.

1 Toast the sliced almonds by placing them in a pre-heated shallow frying pan, then dry-roast by holding the pan above a medium heat for 10–15 seconds and shaking it to prevent burning. The almonds should just begin to turn a slightly brown colour. Remove them from the pan immediately and transfer them to a large dish to cool. Set to one side while preparing the bananas.

2 Chop the bananas coarsely and mix in the lemon juice.

3 Place the flour in a mixing bowl with the spices, sugar and salt. Mix all of the ingredients well and add the bananas.

4 Beat the eggs and gradually add the milk while still beating. Add the egg/milk mixture to the bananas, stirring carefully until the bananas are fully coated.

5 Heat the oil over a medium heat and put in as many large spoonfuls as the pan will hold in a single layer. Fry until the fritters are brown on both sides. Drain on absorbent kitchen paper.

6 Transfer the fritters to a serving plate and brush evenly with the apricot glaze.

7 If using apricot jam instead, heat the jam gently in a ladle or small pan until it just begins to bubble, then push it through a sieve (strainer) before brushing over the fritters.

8 Serve with a dollop of whipped cream and top with a few toasted almonds. Alternatively, vanilla ice cream can be served with the dish for a cooling summer treat.

Index